4   **Contents**

Introduction   **6**

1   **What is type?** ———————— **8**

1.1   **Type today**
Type around us ——————— 10
Using type today ——————— 12
The need for type ——————— 16

1.2   **The development of type**
The first types ———————— 18
Western beginnings ————— 20

1.3   **A brief history of type**
The spread from Mainz ———— 22
The influence of Italy ———— 24
European development ———— 26
Towards the modern ————— 28

1.4   **Case study 1: Francesco Griffo:**
Punch-cutter ———————— **30**

1.5   **Describing type**
Terminology ————————— 32
Basic type anatomy ————— 34

1.6   **Task 1: Serifs** ——————— **36**

2   **Type genealogy** ————— **38**

2.1   **Keep it in the family**
Type, typeface, font ————— 40
Type families ———————— 42
Roman ——————————— 44
Italic ———————————— 46
Variants —————————— 48

2.2   **Distant relations**
Hidden characters – ligatures
and symbols ————————— 50
Expert or pro fonts—————— 52
Extended and super families —— 54

2.3   **Case study 2: Adrian Frutiger**
and Univers ———————— **56**

2.4   **What's in a name?**
Naming conventions ————— 58
Systems of classification ——— 60
The Vox system ——————— 62
The ATypI and British
Standards systems —————— 64
The German DIN system
and others ————————— 66

2.5   **Task 2: Is there a need to**
reclassify? ———————— **68**

3   **Type in context** ————— **70**

3.1   **General types**
Text types ————————— 72
Display types ———————— 76

3.2   **Case study 3: Fiona Ross and**
non-Latin types —————— **78**

3.3   **Type relationships**
Harmonious types —————— 80
Contrasting types——————— 82
Awkward types ———————— 84
Types to avoid———————— 86

3.4   **Seeing is believing**
Legibility —————————— 88
Readability ————————— 90

3.5   **Choosing types – what to**
consider
Selecting text typefaces ——— 92
Selecting display typefaces —— 96

3.6   **Task 3: Appropriateness**——— **98**

4 **Old, new and familiar faces** ——— **100**

4.1 **Regular types**
Fashionable types ——————— 102
Ubiquitous types ——————— 104
Delicate types ———————— 106
Classic types ————————— 108
Real workhorses ——————— 110

4.2 **Genuine types**
Originals —————————— 112
Revivals —————————— 114

4.3 **Case study 4: The Garamonds –** **116**

4.4 **Unique types**
Challenging types —————— 118
Exotic types ———————— 120
Fun types ————————— 122
Unusual types ———————— 124
Future types ————————— 126

4.5 **Finding type**
Books and printed samples ——— 128
Digital sources ——————— 130

4.6 **Task 4: Old and new** ——— **132**

5 **Identifying type** ————— **134**

5.1 **Type spotting**
Which type is which? ————— 136
Playing the detective————— 138
Distinguishing features ———— 140
Putting a face to the name——— 142

5.2 **Case study 5: Erik Spiekermann,**
a life in type ——————— **144**

5.3 **Genetically modified types**
Same face, different names —— 146
Copycats and lookalikes ——— 148

5.4 **Task 5: A few good types** —— **150**

6 **Type and technology** ——— **152**

6.1 **The big reunion**
Designers and type,
together again ———————— 154

6.2 **Case study 6: Jeremy Tankard:**
digital font design ————— **156**

6.3 **Common type formats**
PostScript and TrueType ——— 158
OpenType —————————— 160
Web open font format (WOFF) — 162

6.4 **Task 6: OpenType functions** —— **164**

Conclusion ————————— **166**
Bibliography ———————— **168**
Glossary ————————— **170**
Index ——————————— **174**
Acknowledgements————— **176**
Working with ethics————— **177**

What is type? What is a typeface? What is a font? Are they the same things? What is a type family? What is a type collection? How do you go about choosing a typeface for a design project? Where do you find fonts and where did the designs come from? What's wrong with using only the fonts on my personal computer or downloading free fonts from the web? Why do so many typefaces look the same? What's the difference between type and lettering?

If you are going to use type in a design project, then you will probably have quite a few questions to ask.

Whether you specialize in typography as a subject in itself or you use type within your work as part of a wider subject discipline such as graphic design or communication design, there is a lot to consider when selecting type. It is not simply based upon personal taste or whim. Knowing more about what type is and how it works will inform your practice and improve your work.

As a designer it is your duty or responsibility to know what it is you are working with and to demonstrate sound rationale for design decision-making. If you work with type, then it's only right that you should make it your business to find out enough about it to make informed decisions.

This book does not set out to give a view of the subject of typography as practice, but to look at the basic components used to create typographic matter – namely type. This book will help you get to grips with understanding type and to put this knowledge into practical use. It is not intended as an extended history of letter and type-form, although historical references are necessary in order to illustrate how we have arrived at today's 'typo-landscape' and to consider where this might lead us in the future.

When we work with type, the typefaces we select give voice or 'timbre' to our designed compositions. They can play a dominant role or remain quiet and subdued, resolute or perfunctory in their duty to deliver language in its visual form (and more besides). Yet, when it comes to choosing or working with type, many decisions are made purely on an emotional basis.

We can say that type has personality, so perhaps it is no coincidence that we respond to this in an emotional way through the choices we make. But how can we be sure that our type selection is going to read well at small sizes? Have we given enough consideration to how appropriate the type is for the given problem? Can our emotional response lead us to make poor selections? Perhaps even clichéd?

If you want to know more about the difference between Bodoni and Bembo; why Arial is not the same as Helvetica and what alternatives to consider; what types to respect and what types to avoid, then you will discover some of those answers here.

This book is about looking closer at what most take for granted. Once hooked, it will be very difficult to see type in the same way again.

'When a type design is good it is not because each individual letter of the alphabet is perfect in form, but because there is a feeling of harmony and unbroken rhythm that runs through the whole design, each letter kin to every other and to all.'
Frederic Goudy

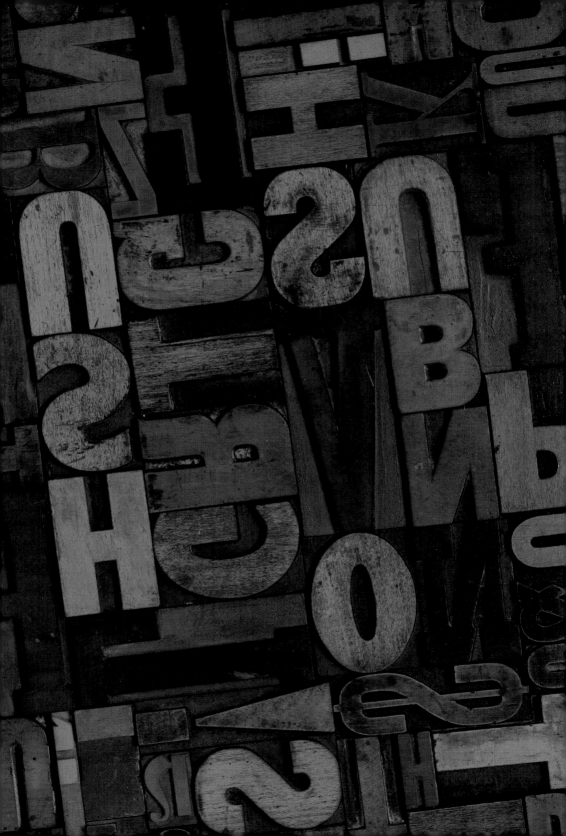

Chapter 1
What is type?

Type is not typography! However, the two are often confused. Typography is concerned with the arrangement of letters and words so that they can be reproduced in print and electronic form. Type can be described as the matter, the composition of typography: the individual letters and symbols and, most importantly, those letters and symbols in relation to the technology that allows for their delivery and use.

Early type required letters and symbols to be fashioned on steel punches by specialist punch-cutters. These punches would be struck into a softer metal, such as copper or brass, in order to produce a matrix that could be placed within a mould. A lead alloy was then poured into the mould to make the type.

Today we may take type for granted because of its seamless integration within modern technical applications. It can be argued that type itself is a technology. This chapter will discuss the development of type and define some of its key characteristics.

Type around us

Type pervades almost every aspect of our day-to-day lives. We interact with it consciously and subconsciously, passively and actively, without giving too much thought to what it is or how it came to be. For most of us type is just 'there'. Yet type is subtly or overtly influencing us in terms of what or how a text is communicated. We decode the inherent semiotic values of the typeforms or overall 'colour' or 'texture' of the text type. Ultimately, we are simultaneously reading both form and content when it comes to visualized language.

Type can set the tone of the page we are reading, be it for single designs or multi-page publications such as books or websites. It can fill the streets within our busy urban environments. Indeed, within some cities it may initially be a more dominant feature than the architecture itself. Imagine removing such type. It would certainly have a lasting effect, not only on the identity of the spaces for the inhabitants and tourist populations alike, but on how we navigate or negotiate such spaces.

Type, once the preserve of the publisher, printer and designer, has become common to most people within a very short period of time. It is something that a great deal of us are actively engaged in using and making decisions about, selecting and applying in the course of our daily activities.

Fig 1.1

Fig 1.2

**Fig 1.1–1.2:
City signage**
Type not only
functions to help us
navigate our busy
urban environments,
it also becomes part
of the identity of that
environment. Hector
Guimard's early
twentieth-century
lettering for the Paris
Metro, later interpreted
as a typeface, is
synonymous with
the city of Paris.

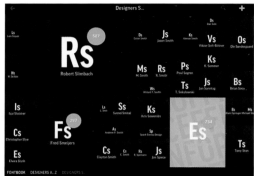

Fig 1.3:
FontBook app
FontShop's FontBook™
app allows users to
discover, explore and
compare types, as well
as their designers, in an
intuitive, seamless user
interface, making for
a compelling
user experience.

Fig 1.3

Using type today

Today, most of us engage with type. Think about creating a new document on your computer: it is almost second nature to choose a different font to the default one. The act of making such choices and then applying them appears to be seamless and effortless thanks to the technologies at our disposal. Or does it?

How do we make these decisions? What kinds of type should be used? What purpose do they serve; what is their intended use?

It is essential for students of graphic design and typography to establish and develop a knowledge of type and put it to effective use within their academic and emerging professional work. Many a promising design has been afflicted with inappropriate or badly considered type, often simply due to a whimsical choice.

For the uninitiated, perhaps the names of types sound interesting; there may be some over-obvious visual association linked to the perception of the design problem at hand; perhaps the reason for such choices is that the type/font could be freely downloaded from the Internet (often solicited by novice type designers, although some very good examples can be found, too). As designers, we have to look beyond the obvious to get to know what works, as well as how and why this is the case. This takes some effort and commitment over time, but the benefit can be the difference between a good and a great piece of work.

As practising professional designers, most of your work will be undertaken for clients, perhaps in the commercial, cultural, public or financial sectors. Your knowledge and ability to select and use type appropriately will say as much about you as a designer as it does about an effective representation of your clients. Subtle as it may seem, type can and does act as the manifestation of the personality of an individual, organization or cause by visual association. Think of some of the most respected, widely read newspapers: without their associated types, their identity would be lost or certainly radically changed.

3069	306A	306B	306C	306D	306E	306F	3070	3071	3072	3073	3074	3075	3076	3077	3078	3079	307A	307B
ど	な	に	ぬ	ね	の	は	ば	ぱ	ひ	び	ぴ	ふ	ぶ	ぷ	へ	べ	ぺ	ほ
307C	307D	307E	307F	3080	3081	3082	3083	3084	3085	3086	3087	3088	3089	308A	308B	308C	308D	308E
ぼ	ぽ	ま	み	む	め	も	ゃ	や	ゅ	ゆ	ょ	よ	ら	り	る	れ	ろ	ゎ
308F	3090	3091	3092	3093	3094	3095	3096	3099	309A	309B	309C	309D	309E	309F	30A0	30A1	30A2	30A3
わ	ゐ	ゑ	を	ん	ゔ	ゕ	ゖ	゙	゚	゛	゜	ゝ	ゞ	ゟ	゠	ァ	ア	ィ
30A4	30A5	30A6	30A7	30A8	30A9	30AA	30AB	30AC	30AD	30AE	30AF	30B0	30B1	30B2	30B3	30B4	30B5	30B6
イ	ゥ	ウ	ェ	エ	ォ	オ	カ	ガ	キ	ギ	ク	グ	ケ	ゲ	コ	ゴ	サ	ザ
30B7	30B8	30B9	30BA	30BB	30BC	30BD	30BE	30BF	30C0	30C1	30C2	30C3	30C4	30C5	30C6	30C7	30C8	30C9
シ	ジ	ス	ズ	セ	ゼ	ソ	ゾ	タ	ダ	チ	ヂ	ッ	ツ	ヅ	テ	デ	ト	ド
30CA	30CB	30CC	30CD	30CE	30CF	30D0	30D1	30D2	30D3	30D4	30D5	30D6	30D7	30D8	30D9	30DA	30DB	30DC
ナ	ニ	ヌ	ネ	ノ	ハ	バ	パ	ヒ	ビ	ピ	フ	ブ	プ	ヘ	ベ	ペ	ホ	ボ
30DD	30DE	30DF	30E0	30E1	30E2	30E3	30E4	30E5	30E6	30E7	30E8	30E9	30EA	30EB	30EC	30ED	30EE	30EF
ポ	マ	ミ	ム	メ	モ	ャ	ヤ	ュ	ユ	ョ	ヨ	ラ	リ	ル	レ	ロ	ヮ	ワ
30F0	30F1	30F2	30F3	30F4	30F5	30F6	30F7	30F8	30F9	30FA	30FB	30FC	30FD	30FE	30FF	3190	3191	3192
ヰ	ヱ	ヲ	ン	ヴ	ヵ	ヶ	ヷ	ヸ	ヹ	ヺ	・	ー	ヽ	ヾ	ヿ	㆐	㆑	㆒
3193	3194	3195	3196	3197	3198	3199	319A	319B	319C	319D	319E	319F	31F0	31F1	31F2	31F3	31F4	31F5
㆓	㆔	㆕	㆖	㆗	㆘	㆙	㆚	㆛	㆜	㆝	㆞	㆟	ㇰ	ㇱ	ㇲ	ㇳ	ㇴ	ㇵ
31F6	31F7	31F8	31F9	31FA	31FB	31FC	31FD	31FE	31FF	3220	3221	3222	3223	3224	3225	3226	3227	3228
ㇶ	ㇷ	ㇸ	ㇹ	ㇺ	ㇻ	ㇼ	ㇽ	ㇾ	ㇿ	㈠	㈡	㈢	㈣	㈤	㈥	㈦	㈧	㈨
3229	322A	322B	322C	322D	322E	322F	3230	3231	3232	3233	3234	3235	3236	3237	3238	3239	323A	323B
㈩	㈪	㈫	㈬	㈭	㈮	㈯	㈰	㈱	㈲	㈳	㈴	㈵	㈶	㈷	㈸	㈹	㈺	㈻
323C	323D	323E	323F	3240	3241	3242	3243	3251	3252	3253	3254	3255	3256	3257	3258	3259	325A	325B
㈼	㈽	㈾	㈿	㉀	㉁	㉂	㉃	㉑	㉒	㉓	㉔	㉕	㉖	㉗	㉘	㉙	㉚	㉛
325C	325D	325E	325F	3280	3281	3282	3283	3284	3285	3286	3287	3288	3289	328A	328B	328C	328D	328E

Fig 1.4

Fig 1.5

Fig 1.4: Digital character set
This detail shows an example of part of a modern digital character set. Each keystroke is assigned a code in order to access the glyph, which resides in the character 'cell'. This can be seen as the digital equivalent of the letterpress type tray.

Fig 1.5: Letterpress type trays
Early type, such as this letterpress wood type, is selected from the type tray. Each tray has specific compartmentalized spaces, within which the types reside.

Fig 1.6

Fig 1.7

Fig 1.6–1.7: Type in the environment
Type must perform in many environments and mediums. From backlit airport signage to high-speed print on low quality newsprint papers, type is often designed for specific purposes. Remaining legible and readable is the optimal function of type in everyday use.

The need for type

The need or demand for type (and the use of it) is undoubtedly greater today than at any other point in history. From printed publications to wayfinding systems, web pages to hand-held mobile devices, the need for type and typography to adapt and develop has increased in recent years. With this has come refinement in the production of type designs: drawings have been refined and redefined; font families have more variants to enable greater accuracy or appropriateness. Many applications of typography require consistency of multilingual settings; this, too, has placed demand upon the development and design of a typeface or font. By way of evidence, we only need compare the variety of basic system fonts that come as standard on personal computers today to those supplied just a few years ago.

The essential need for type, however, is the same today as it was when Gutenberg perfected printing from moveable metal types over 500 years ago. That need was for a mechanized system to deliver the visual representation of language, to allow for the seamless permutation and compilation of characters (or glyphs), which was consistent with the essential aspects of the formal chirographic (handwriting) culture for a given language. That is to say, type, although independent of handwriting, must still retain fundamental characteristics of the written form of language (or groups of languages).

The first types

There is no full, definitive description of the evolution or invention of type. There are traces of invention or part-invention that span many centuries and many locations.

The earliest known moveable types are attributed to the Chinese commoner Bi Sheng, around the middle of the eleventh century during the Song Dynasty. Bi Sheng's types were fashioned from clay, held within a metal frame and adhered to a metal plate by means of resin mixture that was softened by heat to allow the placed characters to be levelled before printing. Although somewhat primitive, Bi Sheng's system involved the essential concept of creating single moveable characters that could be reused and reset.

It is also known that cast-metal (and later, copper and brass) moveable types were in use in Korea in the early thirteenth century, before the introduction of metal types in Europe. The oldest extant book printed from metal type is the Zen Buddhist *Jikji*, printed in two volumes in Korea in 1377. It was added to the UNESCO World Documentary Heritage list in 2001. The sole surviving second volume of the book is held at the Bibliothèque Nationale, France. This pre-dates Gutenberg's 42-line Bible (page 21) by some 78 years.

It is Gutenberg, however, who is widely recognized as having perfected the system of making and casting types, and printing from these onto vellum and paper using oil-based ink via a hand-operated press.

Fig 1.8

Fig 1.9

Fig 1.8: Chinese printing matrix
An example of Chinese clay types similar to those used by Bi Sheng.

Fig 1.9: Chinese moveable type
Some extent of the vast character set required to print Chinese language texts from moveable types can be appreciated in this photograph.

Fig 1.10: Bi Sheng
This image depicts Bi Sheng printing from moveable types. The small type trays on the floor can be seen to be similar to that shown in fig 1.8.

Fig 1.10

1.2
The development of type

Fig 1.11: Metal type
The system of printing from individual reversed types revolutionized Western visual language communication. In principle, this remained largely unchanged for over 500 years.

Fig 1.12: Gutenberg's 42-line Bible
Gutenberg's moveable types allowed him, to a great extent, to emulate the handwritten form of the time, whilst producing the printed pages became much less time consuming than their handwritten counterparts.

Western beginnings

Johannes Gutenberg of Mainz, Germany, created the system that would eventually enable the efficient, cost-effective production of books. He also managed to retain great quality within the work he produced. For the 42-line (or Mazarin) Bible, produced circa 1455, Gutenberg created Textura, a type that was close to the formal handwriting employed in the writing of liturgical texts. It was a rather regimented, Gothic blackletter which, by today's standards, is difficult to read.

Gutenberg produced around 300 variations for characters and ligatures so that the printed letter closely matched the narrow, angular handwritten letterform. In essence, Gutenberg's first types did not explore the possibilities or capabilities of type or typeform independently of handwritten forms; he strove for acceptability, not change. The letterforms of the 42-line Bible evoke authority and austerity, but the angular forms can easily be confused.

In 1460, Gutenberg developed the Catholicon, a small text type that displayed very different qualities to his earlier Textura. Similar in size to today's book type, the shapes of the letterforms were open and rounded and, although these retained a certain Gothic appearance, were more legible than Textura. Around the same time, the practice of printing began to spread rapidly across Europe and with that, the development of type.

Fig 1.11

Fig 1.12

The spread from Mainz

Religious factional fighting and conflict resulted in the sack of the German city of Mainz in 1462, which caused many tradespeople to flee, including those associated with printing. The migration of printers from Germany across Europe brought with it their developing trade and skills. What had been set as precedent for German printing types now had to adapt to national, regional and cultural tastes.

German printers Konrad Sweynheim and Arnold Pannartz set up in Subiaco, Italy using Gutenberg's invention in 1464. Some of their early types, although still Gothic in influence, have a much softer appearance in comparison to the blackletter types of northern Europe; the influence of Italian humanist handwriting can be seen.

The first true roman type was produced in Venice in 1469 by the German brothers Johann and Wendelin da Spira. This type had none of the sharp angles associated with the Gothic types but was instead open and rounded with good clarity and legibility.

Within a year, however, Frenchman Nicolas Jenson, also working in Venice, produced an edition of Eusebius's *De Evangelica Praeparatione* using a roman type so clear, so graceful (particularly the lower case), that to most eyes it would appear as modern as many book types available today.

Centaur

Nunc condimentum purus gravida est auctor eleifend. Nulla eget felis.

QUISQUAM

Fig 1.13

The influence of Italy

In 1495, Italian printer Aldus Manutius and punch-cutter Francesco Griffo (see page 30) developed the so-called Aldine types. These had a great influence on the development of roman types: today we can find typefaces in modern use such as Bembo, first designed under the direction of Stanley Morison in 1929, and Monotype Poliphilus from 1923.

Griffo also cut the first italic type, which appeared in 1501. Although not as widely influential as Arrighi's italics of the 1520s, it is still important to note.

The Aldine types can be seen to influence the work of French typography from around 1532 and in particular, the work of Claude Garamond. Garamond also drew upon the influence of writing master Ludovico Vicentino degli Arrighi. He produced a roman and italic that were related, so treated as members of the same family; what we might see today as the prototype for modern fonts. Prior to this, types only consisted of a single character set or variant and books would be set entirely in either roman or italic.

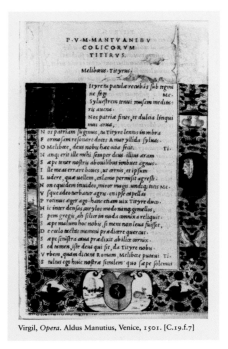

Virgil, *Opera*. Aldus Manutius, Venice, 1501. [C.19.f.7]

Fig 1.14

Fig 1.15

Garamond

At the end of the 19th century the French National Printing Office, founded in 1643 by Cardinal Richelieu, reminded the world through a number of scholarly monumental books that it had been for centuries a great repository of typographical material. In the course of these researches there were brought to light three sets of punches of remarkable beauty and personality. These punches were evidently of an age equal to that of the office itself, and their description, *Caractères de l'Université*, had in the course of centuries also acquired an ascription to Claude Garamond.

When these types were copied by various type-founders after the first world war, they were issued under the name of Garamond; but in 1926 Paul Beaujon's researches in *The Fleuron* identi-fied the designer as Jean Jannon. It was then too late to rename the face, and Jannon remains better known as the printer of a famous minia-ture Bible than as the originator of one of the most popular 20th-century types.

Jannon, a self-taught punch-cutter, was prin-ter to the Calvinist Academy at Sedan. Owing to political disturbances in 1615, he was deprived of his type supplies from Frankfurt and in the space of only six years he cut and struck a magnificent range of sizes. Based on Garamond's models, his design is much lighter and more open and characterized by the sharply-cupped top serifs to some of the letters.

'Monotype' Garamond was the first series to be cut in the ambitious programme of matrix production undertaken by the Corporation in 1922, and it is a close reproduction of Jannon's original. Its early use by the Pelican, Cloister and Nonesuch Presses swiftly made it a "classic", and it is now one of the most widely-used book, periodical and jobbing faces, particularly on the Continent. It is by no means an all-purpose face. Originally designed to stand up to heavy inking and "bash" impression on a damp hand-made paper, it tends to look thin and fussy on coated paper, but it reproduces well by offset.

The italic is taken from a fount of Granjon, which appeared in the repertory of the Imprime-rie Royale and was probably cut in the middle of the 16th century. Its letters are decidedly irregular in slant and steeply inclined, but an alternative, more regularized italic (Series 174) is also available. Both italics are equipped with an extensive range of swash letters and ligatures: a complete range of the 8-point size is shown on the back page. There is also a companion bold face design (Series 201) with one of the best italics available for display work.

Monotype
_{Reg. Trade Mark}

Fig 1.14: Virgil's Opera
Francesco Griffo was the first to produce an italic type. This first appeared in Virgil's *Opera*. In this early work italic type was used for the whole body of the text, with the exception of the capital letters, which were of roman or upright design.

Fig 1.15: Garamond printed sample
Many of the early types have been, and continue to be, revisited and revised, probably none more so than Garamond. However, due to some early misattributions, it was not always the true Garamond types that were being revived.

Baskerville _g_
_c. 1757_
John Baskerville, Birmingham
ENGLAND

Fig 1.16

1798
Giambattista Bodoni
Parma, Italy
Bodoni

Fig 1.17

European development

As printing and typography developed throughout Europe, it can be clearly seen in the shaping of type how each country in turn influenced the others. For example, the sixteenth-century work of Garamond can be seen to influence the seventeenth-century Fell types of Dirk Voskens and the types of Christopher van Dyck of Holland.

Dutch type-founding had great influence in Europe between the seventeenth and eighteenth centuries, before Englishman William Caslon I broke the monopoly of taste for Dutch letter-founding around 1725. Although Caslon's letters were derived from Dutch models, they had an evenness and grace in text settings that made them almost immediately successful. Indeed, his types were even employed in setting the text of the American *Declaration of Independence* of 1776.

Around 1757 John Baskerville published a typeface in which he set out to improve upon the Caslon model. Baskerville's transitional type differed in that the stress or shading of the letters was upright rather than diagonal. Although Baskerville's types were not as immediately successful as Caslon's, they did have their admirers and supporters, namely type-founders Pierre Simon Fournier in France and Giambattista Bodoni in Italy, as well as culturally influential figures such as Benjamin Franklin.

Tastes were changing again, however, and the influences of Philippe Grandjean in France and Johann Michael Fleischmann in Holland had also impacted on the work of Fournier, Didot and Bodoni. From the mid-eighteenth century the modern types increased in popularity.

Fig 1.16: Baskerville
Often classed as a 'transitional' type, Baskerville has a vertical stress to its form.

Fig 1.17: Modern
Continuing the development of the vertical stress, Modern classification types show a much more pronounced or abrupt shading between light and heavy strokes in their form.

Towards the modern

It was perhaps Bodoni's work that established the greatest influence by the turn of the nineteenth century. The variations between thick and thin strokes in some types had a clear influence of copperplate lettering and helped create a new paradigm of type style. These so-called 'fat faces' or 'grotesques' began to have a major influence in Europe and established demand for a new display typography. Along came the Egyptians and Antiques, types that would ultimately form our modern sans serif and slab serif types, along with their derivatives and relatives.

The nineteenth century, and the Industrial Revolution, liberated typography from its book model of old style and modern text types. Types began to explore the romantic, exotic and bizarre. Commerce, travel, advertising and opportunism are reflected in the design and setting of types from this period. In 1816, William Caslon IV created the unassuming Two Lines English Egyptian, a monoline type without serifs, of even weight and shading and shown in upper case only. It was later known as grotesque or Doric. Ultimately, this was the first sans serif as we know it today.

Caslon's type is regarded as the antecedent of such jobbing grotesques as Akzidenz (circa 1890s, also referred to as Berthold and Standard) and the ubiquitous Helvetica (1957). The avant-garde and modernist movements of the early twentieth century helped establish a firm demand for the sans serif. This is exemplified in the early typography of the likes of Jan Tschichold and Paul Renner, through to the Swiss typography of the 1950s and 1960s, which became known as the 'international style'. The influence of these modern movements is still evident today, although somewhat softened and diffused, and we cannot ignore their impact on graphic design and modern book typography.

Fig 1.18

CASLON

Fig 1.19

Fig 1.18: Fat face
Fat-face types became popular as display types. Based upon Moderns, these have even further accentuated contrast between thick and thin elements of their form.

Fig 1.19: Two-Line English Egyptian
The first commercially available sans serif type was William Caslon IV's Two-Line English Egyptian.

Francesco Griffo: Punch-cutter

Also known as Francesco da Bologna, Griffo was a punch-cutter with great talent in the creation of letterforms specifically for use as text typefaces.

Griffo was born circa 1450, around the same time Gutenberg was developing his invention of printing with moveable, metal types. Griffo started out as a goldsmith, which would undoubtedly have helped him develop his skill for working in minute detail. By the end of the fifteenth century he was producing work for the scholarly printer and publisher Aldus Manutius, cutting Greek alphabets.

In 1495 Manutius produced a book of poetry for the poet, and later cardinal, Pietro Bembo entitled *De Aetna*, a 60-page work about a journey to Mount Aetna. The work contained a new roman typeface cut by Griffo, which is now considered to be one of the great model letters, one that Stanley Morison argued became a standard by which other typefaces were developed in Europe over the centuries.

Griffo later refined his roman type in Manutius's 1499 printing of Francesco Colonna's *Hypnerotomachia Poliphili*, regarded as one of most beautiful early printed books. Both type and typography clearly demonstrate the great talents of Griffo and Manutius. Stanley Morison's typeface Monotype Bembo, released in 1929, is based upon Griffo's type for *De Aetna*.

Griffo also developed the first italic typeface, which appeared in Manutius's edition of Virgil's *Opera* (1501). This became very popular due to the scholarly accuracy of the text and the convenient small size of the book. Although technically sound, Griffo's italics did not have the same influence on type design as his roman letters.

These early types, commissioned by Manutius and cut by Griffo, had widespread influence. This was partly due to Manutius's editions being seen as scholarly and correct in terms of content and, therefore, desirable to own and copy.

Fig 1.20

QV ARTVS

LA MVLTITVDINE DEGLI AMANTI GIOVENI, ET
DILLE DIVE AMOROSE PVELLE LA NYMPHA APOLI
PHILO FACVNDAMENTE DECHIARA, CHI FVRO.
NO ET COME DAGLI DII AMATE. ET GLI CHORI DE.
GLI DIVI VATICANTANTI VIDE.

LCVNO MAI DIT ANTO INDEFESSO E LO
quio aptamente se accommodarebbe, che gli diuini ar
chani disertando copioso & pienamente potesse euade
re & uscire. Et expressamente narrare, & cum quanto di
ua pompa, indesinenti Triumphi, perenne gloria, festi
ua lætitia, & fœlice tripudio, circa a queste quatro iuisi
tate seiuge de memorando spectamine cum parole sufficientemente ex-
primere ualesse. Oltra gli inclyti adolescentuli & stipante agmine di inu-
mere & periucunde Nymphe, piu che la tenerecia degli anni sui elle pru-
dente & graue & astutule cum gli acceptissimi amanti de pubescente
& depile gene. Ad alcuni la primula lanugine splendescéte le male in-
serpiua delitiose alacremente festigiauano. Molte hauendo le facole sue
accense & ardente . Alcune uidi Pastophore. . Altre cum drite haste
adornate de prische spolie. Et tali di uarii Trophæi optimaméte ordinate

Francesco Colonna (?), *Hypnerotomachia Poliphili*. Aldus Manutius, Venice, 1499. [86.k.9]

Fig 1.20:
Hypnerotomachia Poliphili
An example from the *Hypnerotomachia Poliphili*, printed by Aldus Manutius in 1499. The types developed by Griffo and Manutius greatly influenced the development of roman types.

Fig 1.21: Type 'zones'
Basic terminology in relation to Western type and the 'zones' that the elements of the letterforms occupy.

Fig 1.22: Type terminology
Terminology as it relates to type variants. Note the distinction that can exist between the 'true' italic, in this example Baskerville, and the slanted or oblique roman that forms the italic of Helvetica.

Terminology

Type, like any subject, has its own language, one that appears to evolve or bend to the persuasions of fashion. There will be times when you will need to keep up to date with this use of 'lingua-typo'. There are, however, some fairly comprehensive and basic terminologies covered on the following pages that should be of benefit, particularly to those new to the subject.

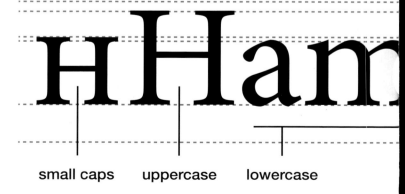

cap height
small caps height

small caps   uppercase   lowercase

Fig 1.21

1. Serif (Baskerville)

2. Roman*Italic*

3. Regular**Semibold**Bold

4. **Sans Serif**(Helvetica Neue)

5. Regular*Oblique*

6. UltraLight**CondensedBlack**

Fig 1.22

purgsx

ascender height

x-height

baseline

descender depth

Basic type anatomy

We have seen how language related to the subject of understanding type in general can be beneficial. Deconstruction of the various letter-parts associated with type will enable a greater understanding and confidence when working with type.

Some of these may have different labels according to time and culture; however, establishing some basics is necessary for the beginner.

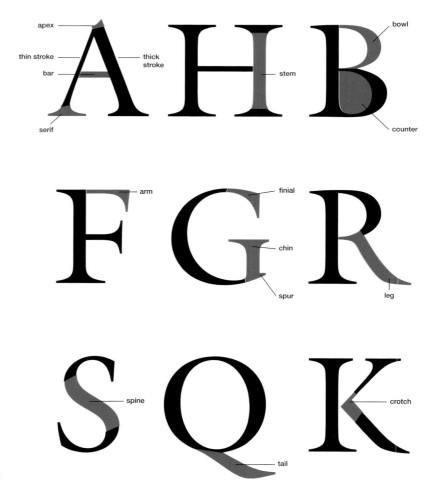

Fig 1.23

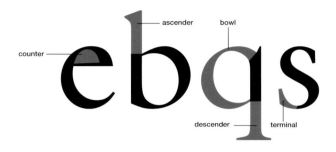

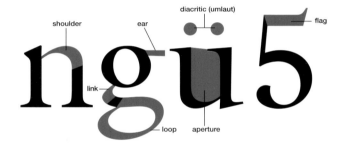

Fig 1.24

**Fig 1.23: Terminology –
upper case**
Some significant
terminology relating
to the parts of the
letters found within
the roman upper-case
(majuscule) form.

**Fig 1.24: Terminology –
lower case**
Significant terminology
relating to the parts of
the letters found within
the roman lower-case
(minuscule) form.

Serifs

There are thousands of typefaces available today. Some of them are modern; many of them are based upon historical models. Many of these types (but not all) fall quite neatly into categories of two: serif and sans serif; text and display types, and so on. Beyond this, things get a little more complicated. It is necessary to dig deeper in order to develop an understanding of type.

Task

Make a collection of 20 different serif typefaces. These can be photographed, photocopied, laser printed or found on your computer – it's up to you.

Once you have 20, see if you can sort them into groups or categories based on the appearance of their serifs. For example, are they flat or curved? Do they have a curve towards the stem or the stroke of the type? Are they tapered or flared? Are they rounded or split in appearance?

Once you have identified your groups, try to be more specific about how you use the correct terminology to describe them. Does this help categorize them further? Does it give you some insight into the period of the type or its influences?

Tip

Try to make your initial selection as diverse as possible. Once you start to see and identify the types and their serifs, you can try to be a little more specific in making your choices for analysis.

Fig 1.25: Serif spotting
Careful examination of serifs and terminals can tell us a lot about a particular typeface. It can help towards identification and grouping in terms of history and classification.

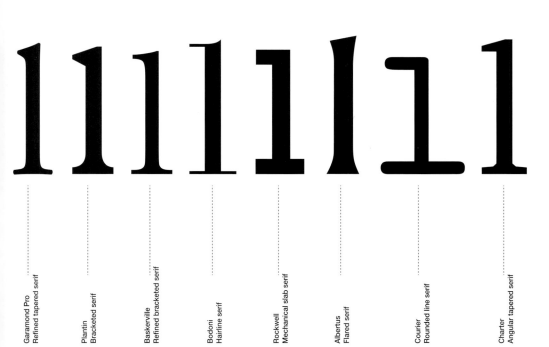

Garamond Pro
Refined tapered serif

Plantin
Bracketed serif

Baskerville
Refined bracketed serif

Bodoni
Hairline serif

Rockwell
Mechanical slab serif

Albertus
Flared serif

Courier
Rounded line serif

Charter
Angular tapered serif

Fig 1.25

Chapter 2
Type genealogy

How does one aspect of the way we describe a typeface relate to another? What are the connections between typefaces and their characteristics? Why are there so many variations of typefaces to choose from and how are their names and groupings arrived at?

Just like looking at our own family histories and genealogy, we can trace connections from the typefaces we use today to their near and distant relatives. Cool, bright young things today may display many traits similar to those of their ancestors. Indeed, some may be complete throwbacks to an earlier generation. There are the high-flyers to be found as well as the meek and mild, the pretentious and the stoic, the hard workers and the eccentric.

Over the years, those with a deep interest in type and typography have attempted to categorize and classify it, even bracket and pigeonhole it, in order to describe and understand its relationships. This chapter looks at some of these relationships and descriptions.

Type, typeface, font

Type and typography have always been bound to technology, from metal type through phototypesetting to today's digital type. Along with developing technologies, the ways in which typefaces have been supplied or grouped have meant that there is often confusion about how we use the terms 'type', 'typeface' and 'font' in relation to the letterforms of typography.

Originally, the word typeface literally meant the face, or printing surface, of metal or wooden type. The term also implied the design or style.

A font – originally a 'fount', also known as a 'fund' of type – referred to a useable collection of types of the same/related design (typeface). This could be found in a tray of type, for example. The term could also be used to describe related types, such as roman, italic and so on.

Today, the term typeface is still used to refer to the design and font is the collected, useable set. With the development of various technologies the term 'families' emerged, offering larger related sets of typefaces – semi-bold, expanded, compressed and so on. The term font, therefore, can represent a single weight/style of typeface (the design), but may also refer to a font family – a set of related weights/styles/variants such as roman, italic, bold, small-caps and semi-bold (a group of related typeface designs).

Fig 2.1

Fig 2.3

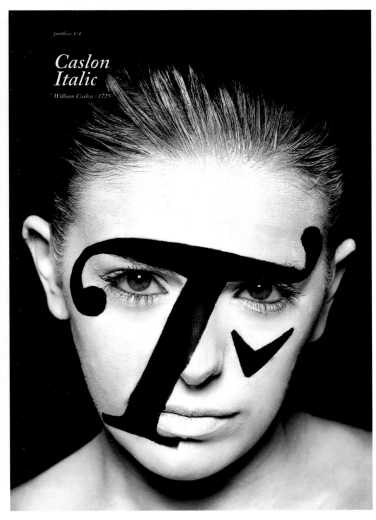

Fig 2.2

Fig 2.1:
Specimen sheet
The early promotion of a
type-founder's types was
presented in sheet form,
showing the quality and
extent of their types.

Fig 2.2–2.3: Fontface
A modern interpretation
of typeface promotion!
Atipo's Fontface series
explores the forms
of classic types in
a playful manner.

Type families

Type families are related sets of typeface designs specifically intended to work with and complement one another. These can be planned and developed from the outset, as is the case with Adrian Frutiger's Univers (see page 56), or developed and added to over a period of time, with varying success, such as the variations and additions to Gill Sans.

Early typefaces were not developed in sets or families but were produced as single weights or versions, mainly for the printing of books. Even when the first italic types appeared around 1501, they were not considered as derivatives or supplements to existing roman types, or as part of a family, but as separate or individual designs.

What might be considered early families were different sizes of the same or similar design. Because there was no way to exactly replicate or scale a design in the early days of type making, differing sizes would inevitably appear optically different, although modelled in the same manner.

The concept of type families is a much more recent phenomenon in type history, examples of which can be found in the mid-nineteenth century. By the early twentieth century the notion of producing types with related but varying weights became more common practice. New technology, such as the pantograph and the Benton punch-cutting machine, no doubt aided the development of the type family. Computers now blend or interpolate between different typeface weights and styles to produce variations.

Today, type families may include differences in optical sizes, weights, widths and designs – roman, italic, Latin, non-Latin, and so on. Type 'family' may not be a very accurate descriptor, but it is one that we can use to identify groups of intentionally related designs.

u u u u
u u u u
u u u u
uu*nivers*

Fig 2.4

Fig 2.5

Fig 2.4: Univers
Adrian Frutiger's Univers typeface was conceived to work as a harmonized family of variants from the outset. It was the first of its kind to take a modular approach to assigning weights and variants based upon a grid-like system.

Fig 2.5: Ardoise
Modern type families, such as Ardoise by Jean Francois Porchez, contain many variants and alternative characters within those variants, offering great flexibility to typographers today.

Roman

With respect to type and typefaces, the term 'roman' has a somewhat ambiguous meaning. Loosely, the word refers to the quality or variant of a typeface that is seen as its normal or regular form. It also generally applies to the upright characteristics of the type; to the regular nature of upright, incised roman capital letters, such as those inscribed on Trajan's Column, a momument erected in Rome in 113 AD. However, it is also linked to the early forms of Italian typefaces that developed from models of Italian humanist handwriting.

Early forms of roman types have been described as Venetian or humanist. These include examples such as Nicolas Jenson's 1470 archetypal typeface produced for Eusebius's *De Praeparatione Evangelica* and Francesco Griffo's type cut for *De Aetna* circa 1495 (see also page 30). This latter type (and developments of it) was used as the inspiration for Stanley Morison's Bembo, which was released in 1929.

The distinctions between the model letters of Jenson – often referred to as Venetian – and those of Griffo – often referred to as Aldine or old-style – are subtle to most. Venetians tend to have a definite oblique axis or stress in the rounded characters within the typeface, old-styles very slightly less so. This can be difficult to detect. Another prominent feature of Venetian types is the diagonal crossbar found on the lower-case 'e'. In old-style types this appears horizontal.

Whether serif, sans serif, humanist, old-style, transitional or modern, most Western types are divided into the loose categories of roman (upright) and italic.

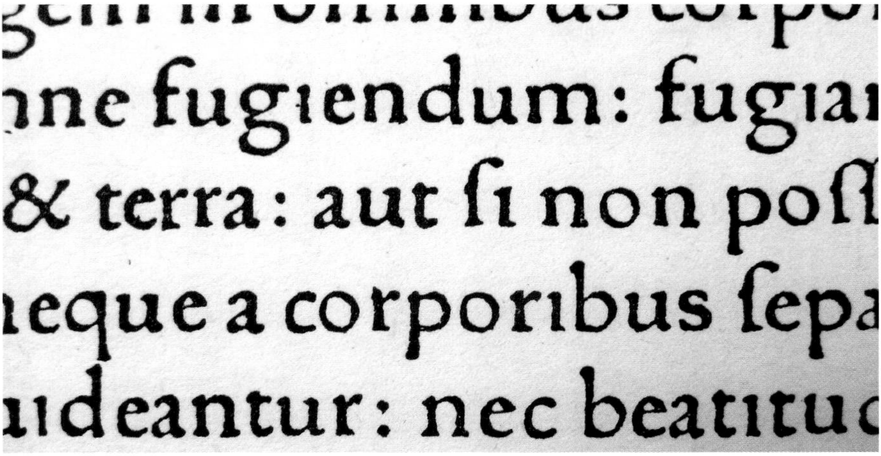

Fig 2.6

Fig 2.7

Fig 2.6: The first 'roman' type
Johann and Wendelin da Spira were amongst the first to introduce printing to Italy from Mainz, Germany. Their roman type emulated the Italian humanist handwriting of the period.

Fig 2.7: Roman type today
Today, roman type has to be able to withstand many different applications, from books to newspapers, and posters to web pages. This example shows the versatile FF More from FontShop.

2.1

Keep it in the family

Italic

Italic types are predominantly slanted or sloping in form (although more upright versions do exist), with unilateral serifs where these form part of the design. Italic variants of today's typefaces are normally designed as true italics: related but distinguished as different to their roman counterparts. This relationship can be traced back to the earliest forms of roman and italic types that coexisted but were independent of each other. Italic forms should not be confused with forced italics, which can be produced in some software programs, or oblique versions of roman typefaces.

The italic type or Aldino, first produced by Francesco Griffo for Aldus Manutius, had a sloping or cursive lower case alongside roman or upright initial capitals. Manutius's italic types were soon copied by other printers, most notably those in Lyon, France, and it is within these later works that the italic capital appears.

Fig 2.8: The first 'italic' type
This example shows Francesco Griffo's first italic type. To our eyes today this appears rather heavy and dense.

Fig 2.9: Dolly
Underware's Dolly, though not a revival typeface, draws upon history in its influence. Many modern types can be seen to have a more balanced relationship with respect to their roman and italic variants.

Francesco Griffo's italic was quite a compact and dense letter, the form of which was improved upon by the designs of Ludovico Arrighi circa 1527, and the calligrapher Tagliente in 1532.

These later designs, particularly in the case of Arrighi, are close to the italic types we are familiar with today.

Early italic types were used separately, as typefaces in their own right, until the mid-sixteenth century when their use began to be limited within a book's preliminaries. These settings use italic for stress, emphasis and highlighting, much as we would expect to see today.

Fig 2.8

> **L** umina, labentem cœlo quæ ducitis annum
> **L** iber, et almâ Ceres, uestro si munere tellus
> **C** haoniam pingui glandem mutauit arista,
> **P** oculaq; inuentis Acheloia miscuit uuis,
> **E** t uos agrestum præsentia numina Fauni,
> **F** erte simul, Fauniq; pedem, Dryadesq; pue

Fig 2.9

Hidden characters – ligatures and symbols

Today, we are mostly unaware of the hidden characters that make up a font. In the days of metal and wood typesetting – especially that set by hand – the material nature of any type could be seen, as it was laid out within specially arranged type trays. Today's computer keyboards show only basic characters, numerals and punctuation, and upper-case or lower-case sets for the main keys.

Again, these would have been clear to those working in metal or wood types: the terms upper case and lower case derive from the practice of composing type, where the printing types would be laid out in trays or cases. Two trays would contain large letters (majuscule) and associated forms, and small letters (minuscule) and associated forms. The trays would be arranged one above the other on the workbench, with majuscules in the upper case and minuscules in the lower case.

This is influenced by the history of the development of Western typography and the language bases that it served. Many languages have character sets that are unicase, which means they have only one set.

Standard hidden characters we might find within fonts today include ligatures or joined letter combinations for fi, fl, ff, ffi and ffl. There are also many diacritical marks, or accents, and a limited number of mathematical and scientific characters.

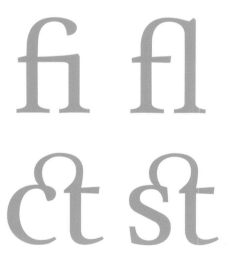

Fig 2.12

Fig 2.13

Fig 2.12: Ligatures
Examples of
standard (above) and
discretionary (below)
ligatures that may
appear within a typeface
character set.

**Fig 2.13: Collective
identity**
The ligature forms
an interesting but
significant focal point
in this exhibition identity
design, created by
the author.

Small caps	ABCDEFGH	Fig 2.14
Old style figures	1234567890	
Lining figures	1234567890	
Ligatures	fi fl ff ffi ffl	
Discretionary ligatures	Th ct ffk sþ	
Multi-language support	ж щ ю ħ	
Fractions	½ ⅓ ¼ ⅛	
Maths	√ ≠ π ω	
Currency	£ $ ¢ ¥ ƒ	
Extras	e m r	

Arabic لاتينية   Fig 2.15

Arabic لاتينية

Arabic لاتينية

Arabic لاتينية

Latin & Arabic in harmony   حروف لاتينية وعربية متناسقة

Latin & Arabic in harmony   حروف لاتينية وعربية متناسقة

Latin & Arabic in harmony   حروف لاتينية وعربية متناسقة

Latin & Arabic in harmony   حروف لاتينية وعربية متناسقة

Expert or pro fonts

Modern typefaces and fonts include additional characters to those that are hidden within a standard set. The OpenType format allows type designers to include additional characters that may afford complex or detailed typographic setting. Such sets of characters that extend an existing typeface are referred to as expert sets; those from the extended OpenType glyph pallet may be referred to as 'pro fonts'.

OpenType enables cross-platform use of typefaces, which means they can be used on Macintosh, PC and Unix computers. They also offer a much larger glyph set than previous standards such as PostScript Type 1 and TrueType fonts. These latter font formats allowed up to 256 characters, whereas OpenType allows for up to 65,000 glyphs, which has greatly increased the possibilities for the use of a single font file. The Unicode encoding of languages such as Chinese, Japanese and Korean, for example, can be accommodated much more efficiently with OpenType than would have been possible with the smaller character sets of PostScript and TrueType.

OpenType also allows software programs to manage or detail certain attributes. For example, a pro font may offer lining and non-lining numerals for tabular or in-line text setting, respectively. OpenType enables certain software programs to switch features on and off, enabling greater choice and manageability.

Fig 2.14: OpenType
OpenType allows type designers to create expert sets of characters to be included within one font file, rather than having separate files to allow for the likes of those glyphs shown here. These are commonly termed 'pro' fonts.

Fig 2.15: Non-Latins
Due to the extensive number of characters that can now be included within a font design, OpenType is ideally suited to the development of non-Latin types.

Fig 2.16–2.17:
Super Families
Super families can
not only contain an
extensive range of
variants in terms
of weights and widths,
they may also include
related type styles as
family members such
as serif, sans serif,
slab serif, Latin and
non-Latin versions.

Examples shown are:
Fig 2.16: FF More and
FF Good; and Fig 2.17:
FF Amman Sans and
Serif. All from FontShop
international.

Extended and super families

An extended typeface family may
include variants that go beyond
the standard version, forming a
comprehensive set of types. A standard
font family may consist of roman,
italic and bold variants. An extended
family may also have additional bold
italic, semi-bold, semi-bold italic and
condensed variants.

A super family, however, may contain
a much greater range of variants and
associated or related styles. These
can belong to single classification
styles as well as variants from different
classifications. For example, a super
family may be a sans serif-only family
with an exhaustive set of variants
that include variations in width
(compressed, extended) and weight
(ultra-light to heavy). They may also
contain related variants such as serif
(roman), sans, slab serif and semi-serif,
therefore offering a set of packaged
typefaces that are both versatile and
durable. Super families may be either
intentionally related designs or those
that have evolved over a longer period.

Some notable examples include Lucas
de Groot's 1994 Thesis, which led the
way for many other modern super
families. It included three type versions:
sans, serif and semi-sans, each of which
had eight weights and each weight had
six variants; it totalled 144 fonts when
initially released. It is probably Adrian
Frutiger's Univers typeface however,
that many see as the progenitor of
modern super families.

Fig 2.16

Fig 2.17

Adrian Frutiger and Univers

Adrian Frutiger is one of the most notable and respected type designers of the twentieth and twenty-first centuries. He has designed more than 50 typefaces and influenced the direction of modern type design and typography.

It was with his typeface Univers – released by the French type foundry Deberny & Peignot, in 1957 – that Frutiger gained worldwide attention.

Charles Peignot was keen to release a sans serif font family similar to the Bauer foundry's Futura, which would work in photocomposition and in metal type. Frutiger argued that the geometric form and spacing of Futura was not in keeping with the times, and that the current practice was to set sans serif types tighter than in the past. This meant that the spaces within the letters (the counters) appeared larger than the spaces around the letters (the side bearings), resulting in the need to reconsider the relationships of rhythm and form.

Frutiger's Univers was developed as a relational system of types around a horizontal and vertical axis of weights and widths. The result was a family of 21 variants that ranged from extra light to black in weight and from extra condensed to extended widths. Univers also included a system of numbers that were used to describe the characteristics of the types, much like those found in the periodic table. The result was a clean, modern unified type system that found immediate approval. It has been argued that, of all the versions of Univers produced down the years, the best is the metal version originally cast by Deberny & Peignot.

Fig 2.18

Fig 2.19

Naming conventions

It has already been mentioned that within the realms of type and typography many words or phrases are shared or misattributed. Type language is useful, if not essential, to help us make sense of what we are working with and how we understand it in relation to type.

Font names can appear to be somewhat inconsistent or arbitrary. Although there are many descriptive terms associated with typefaces and fonts, many of these can also become muddled. There are no strict naming conventions and so familiarity is important; just spending time observing the different ways in which things are described helps us understand how certain generic factors or attributes may be found within the design or look and feel of types.

There are some attributes of any typeface design or font that can help us search for clarity:

- First, the typeface's given name;
- Secondly, we can describe its variant style: roman, italic, small caps and so on;
- Thirdly, the weight, whether it is light, bold, regular and so on.

Naming conventions related to the classification of types can also help us to understand and communicate the nature of the type forms, their link to history and their purpose of use. But this, too, is not always clear.

Light *Light Italic*
Regular *Italic*
Semibold *Semibold Italic*
Bold ***Bold Italic***
Bold Condensed

Light
Regular *Italic*
Medium ***Medium Italic***
Bold ***Bold Italic***
Super

45 Light *46 Light Oblique*
55 Regular *56 Oblique*
65 Bold ***66 Bold Oblique***
75 Black ***76 Black Oblique***

Fig 2.20

Fig 2.20: Common family variant names There is no consensus upon which variants are named. Confusion between italic and oblique is common, as well as medium, semi-bold and demi-bold. Familiarity with these terms will come with practise.

Systems of classification

There have been several attempts to classify types into orderly groups or sets in order to gain a better sense of their form, history and context.

It is very useful to have even a basic knowledge of these broad terms of classification. It helps identify the kind of typeface we are looking at, explore its origins and discover its precedents in the development of the design.

Most type classification systems offer a linear or chronological approach in line with the historical development of typefaces. Some offer broad and useful categorizations, but may have an assumption that the user of such classification systems already knows the categories within which to place type designs.

As new classification systems have developed – some building upon existing models, some with the ambition to supplant pre-existing attempts – there is a recurring theme that no one system is ideal. However, a working knowledge of the history and development of types, and their related letterforms and attributes, is essential for any practising typographer or graphic designer.

Some classification systems are simple in their approach, others are more meticulous in definition and detail, and while none is really an aid to selecting types, they all help contextualize them.

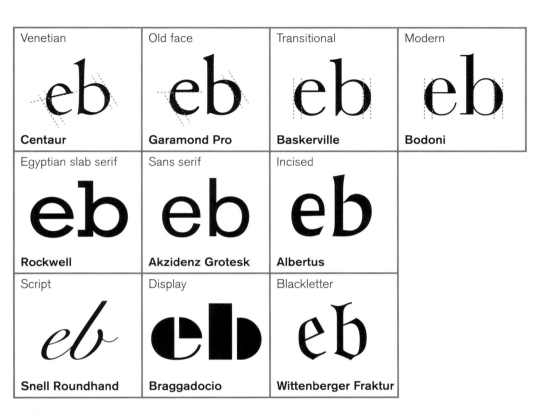

Venetian	Old face	Transitional	Modern
Centaur	**Garamond Pro**	**Baskerville**	**Bodoni**
Egyptian slab serif	Sans serif	Incised	
Rockwell	**Akzidenz Grotesk**	**Albertus**	
Script	Display	Blackletter	
Snell Roundhand	**Braggadocio**	**Wittenberger Fraktur**	

Fig 2.21

Fig 2.21: Types of type
A general approach to type classification can be a good place to start and will aid in familiarization of types in terms of history and development.

Designer and typographer Maximilien Vox began work on a typeface classification system that was eventually published in 1954 and is probably the most influential system to date. Vox was influenced by an earlier classification system, created in 1921 by the French typographer Francis Thibaudeau, which divided types into four main categories dependent upon shape and character of the serif.

The Vox system contained nine categories of classification:

- Manuaires – types inspired by lettering of the Middle Ages.
- Humanes – types inspired by Italian Renaissance humanist forms.
- Garaldes – types resembling classical forms, such as those of Garamond and Aldus Manutius.
- Réales – types resembling rationalist eighteenth-century forms.
- Didones – types resembling nineteenth-century forms, such as those of Didot and Bodoni.
- Mécanes – types with a geometric or mechanical appearance.
- Linéales – types with regular stroke width, modern typographic forms without serifs.
- Incises – types that resemble monumental stone carved letters.
- Scriptes – types that resemble handwriting.

Although the Vox system generally followed the historical development of archetypal typefaces through the centuries, many type designs would not conveniently fall into one category alone, often needing to draw from two or more descriptions.

Fig 2.22

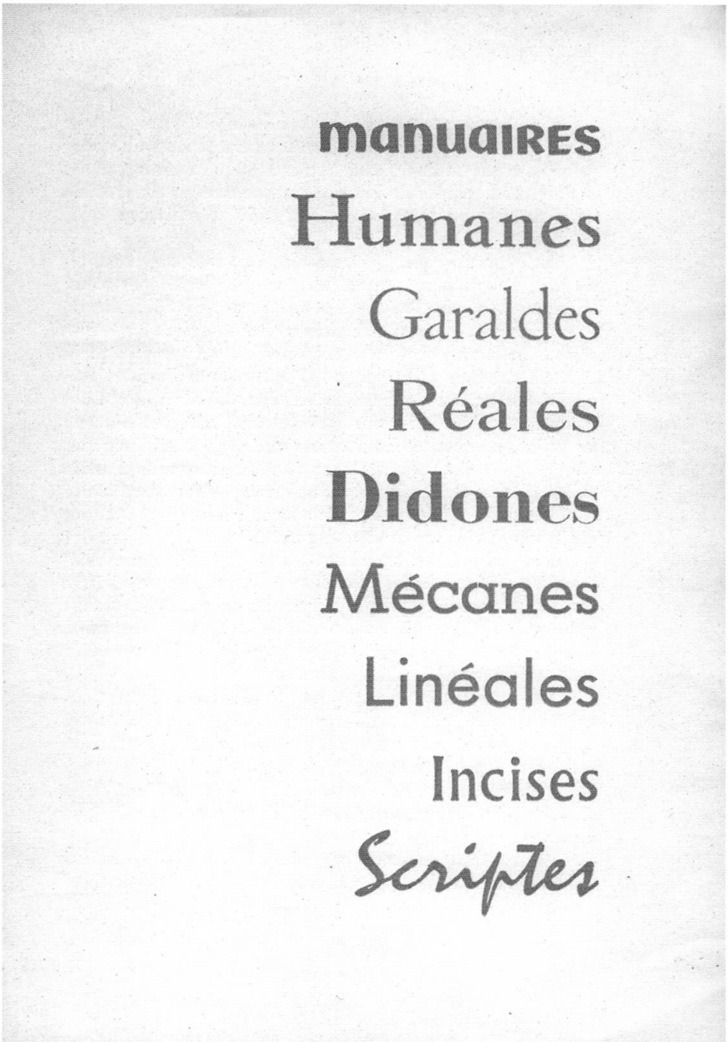

Fig 2.23

manuaiREs

Humanes

Garaldes

Réales

Didones

Mécanes

Linéales

Incises

Scriptes

Fig 2.22: Mapping the Vox system
This diagram, illustrated by Jean Francois Porchez and based on Vox's original hand-drawn version, shows examples of types in relation to classification groups.

Fig 2.23: Vox system
An example of the approach to type classification developed by Maximilien Vox.

The ATypI and British Standards systems

Despite any shortcomings of the Vox system today, it continues to prove useful as a contained system of typeface description. The benefits of the Vox system were acknowledged by the Association Typographique Internationale (ATypI), when they adopted it in 1962. ATypI added two further categories to the system (in French):

- Fractura – blackletter types
- Orientale – non-Latin types

As an international society, the English translation of the Vox-ATypI system appeared as follows:

- Venetian
- Old face
- Transitional
- Modern face
- Egyptian slab serif
- Sans serif
- Incised Latin
- Scripts
- Hand-drawn types/display types
- Blackletter
- Non-Latin

In 1967 the Vox-ATypI system was adopted in the UK as a British Standard or BS (the British Standards Classification of Typefaces BS 2961). The BS version was an interpretation of the Vox-ATypI system, which retained three of the original Vox names and expanded upon the Lineal category to broaden the description of sans serif types, probably as a response to their rise in popularity at the time.

The ATypI classification system is as follows:

1 Classicals
    1.1 Humanist
    1.2 Garalde
    1.3 Transitional

2 Moderns
    2.1 Didone
    2.2 Mechanistic
    2.3 Lineal
        2.3.1 Grotesque
        2.3.2 Neo-grotesque
        2.3.3 Geometric
        2.3.4 Humanist

3 Calligraphics
    3.1 Glyphic
    3.2 Script
    3.3 Graphic
    3.4 Blackletter
    3.5 Gaelic

The realization was that the system remained unsatisfactory: terms such as transitional were not ideal; lineal and sans serif were subdivided but other categories were not. It is acknowledged that both the Vox-ATypI and the BS system have large gaps in their constructions. In 2010 ATypI introduced an additional category of Gaelic to the calligraphic group. The BS version has since been withdrawn.

Fig 2.24

Humanist (Centaur)

Garalde (Garamond Pro)

Transitional (Baskerville)

Didone (Bauer Bodoni)

Slab serif (Rockwell)

Lineal: Grotesque (Akzidenz Grotesk)

Neo Grotesque (Helvetica)

Geometric (Futura)

Humanist (Gill Sans)

Glyphic (Albertus)

Script (Snell Roundhand)

Graphic (Braggadocio)

Fig 2.24: BS Classification
The British Standards Classification of Typefaces shown with example types set.

The German DIN system and others

A national standard for type classification was adopted by the German Institute for Standardization (DIN) as Standard 16518 in 1964. Like its counterparts, the German system is partly obsolete and many new typefaces are difficult to categorize. However, the DIN 1451 type classification, which was founded in 1936 and used for technology, traffic, businesses and street signs, has had a lasting effect on national and international design culture.

Other systems, such as the PANOSE, enable the identification of typefaces based on visual appearance. In 1985 Benjamin Bauermeister developed a system that was published in 1988 as *A Manual of Comparative Typography: The PANOSE System*. The original version contained seven categories relating to visual parameters. Today, the system comprises ten visual comparative categories, each of which is numbered. The system has been developed into PANOSE Mapper software, which contains a database of known fonts – each identified by a sequence of category numbers – and determines the closest possible match to any given typeface.

There have been other notable attempts to produce classification systems. These include Italian type designer Aldo Novarese's 1964 proposal with categories Renaissance Antiqua, Baroque Antiqua, Classic Antiqua, Serifless Stressed Linear Antiqua, Serifless Linear, Antique Variants/Scripts and Handwritten/Broken Scripts.

Type designer Marcel Jacno's 1978 classification system included only four categories; Linéale, Ancient Roman, Modern Roman and Egyptian. In 1979, fellow French designer Jean Antoine Alessandrini sought to radically change existing typographic terminology with his system, which comprised 19 categories.

In more recent years a proposal from Robert Bringhurst identified periods of major typographic developments that relate to significant artistic and cultural development in general.

Designer, researcher and tutor Dr Catherine Dixon's PhD research also developed a system of classification, one that describes type based upon two main components: sources (generic influences) and formal attributes (specific formal characteristics).

Whatever system may prevail in the future, some knowledge of even the most basic systems of type classification is useful.

Attribute	Setting	Class No.
Family kind	Latin text	2
Serif style	Cove	2
Weight	Medium	6
Proportion	Modern	3
Contrast	Medium low	5
Stroke variation	Transitional	4
Arm style	Straight arms	5
Letterform	Round	2
Midline	Standard	3
X-height	Large	4

Times New Roman
2263545234

Fig 2.25

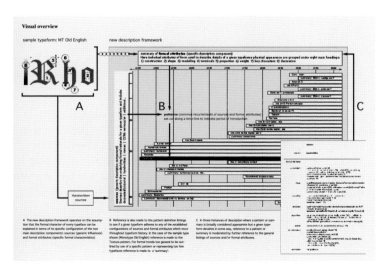

Fig 2.26

Fig 2.25: PANOSE
An example of the PANOSE identification system, showing Times New Roman.

Fig 2.26: Dixon system
An excerpt from an overview of Catherine Dixon's type description framework, developed from her PhD research.

Is there a need to reclassify?

As we have seen, there are many examples of type classification systems. Some are adaptations, simplifications or syntheses of other systems. In contrast, some approaches have been entirely new, perhaps ignoring the historical development of type or the accepted, conventional use of typographic nomenclature.

There is no firm agreement or definitive system, so it makes sense to develop a personal understanding, which should include awareness of some of the systems used and proposed by others.

Task

A simplified version of the categories for a type classification system may appear as follows:

- Venetian
- Old style
- Transitional
- Modern
- Slab serif
- Sans serif
- Incised
- Handwritten
- Graphic

Using this system, find three typefaces that relate to each category. For some, you will need to check details within the type design relating to stress or axis. The shape and form of serifs (or lack of serifs) will need to be considered for others. Perhaps the typefaces you find will fit into historical archetypes.

Once you have categorized the types, note your reasoning for each decision.

It often takes some time to be able to identify the essential characteristics of types and it is easy to see why the notion of classification is an attractive proposition.

Tip

Check the types that you find against the simplified table of categories given on page 61. Finding out about the history of the type that you identify can also help with the notion of how a type may be described or classified.

Fig 2.27: Template Gothic

Barry Deck's Template Gothic typeface used within the challenging but seminal *Émigré* magazine. Which classification group would this comfortably reside within?

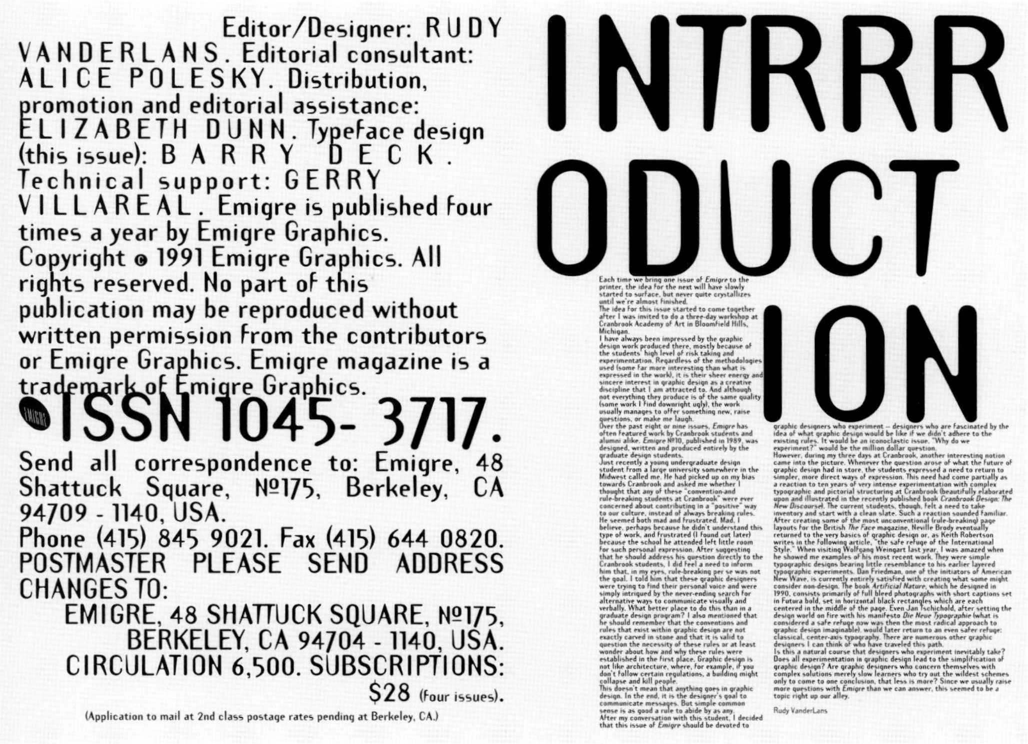

Fig 2.27

SHORT NOTICE OF SALE.

AUCTION ROOMS

Melville Street, Ryde.

SALE OF MODERN HOUSEHOLD FURNITURE.

MESSRS.

WALLIS, RIDDETT & DOWN

WILL SELL BY AUCTION, AT THEIR LARGE SALE ROOMS, AS ABOVE,

ON TUESDAY, JULY 12TH, 1881,

AT ONE O'CLOCK PUNCTUALLY, ABOUT

200 LOTS

OF HOUSEHOLD

FURNITURE

AND EFFECTS, INCLUDING:

BRUSSELS, TAPESTRY & FELT CARPETS,

Brass and Iron Fenders and Fire Implements, Rep, Damask and Muslin Window Curtains, Sewing Machines, Bronzed-iron two-tier Table,

MAHOGANY, OAK & WALNUT BOOKCASES,

Walnut Loo Tables, Mahogany Chiffonniere, Chimney Glasses in gilt frames, Sofa Ottomans, Couches and Easy Chairs,

TWO POLISHED PINE WARDROBES,

Mahogany Chests of Drawers, Washstands, Dressing Tables and Glasses, a well-made Japanned-oak Hanging Wardrobe,

BRASS & IRON FRENCH BEDSTEADS,

with Bedding, including several good Feather Beds,

A LIGHT-RUNNING PHAETON,

AND NUMEROUS OTHER EFFECTS.

THE ABOVE MAY BE VIEWED ON THE PRECEDING DAY AND MORNING OF SALE.

Catalogues at Messrs. WALLIS, RIDDETT & DOWN'S Auction and Valuation Offices, Ryde.

Chapter 3
Type in context

Why does one kind of typeface work well for text, making the reading experience smooth and pleasant, while other types seem to fight for attention? What is the difference between the kinds of types we use for text settings and those chosen for display?

Relationships are not always easy to get right. Sometimes we can feel awkward and embarrassed to stand next to someone; sometimes it feels like you've known that person all your life. Getting the balance right with type – what we select, the way we combine types, working out which is the dominant character – can feel almost like we're dealing with real-life relationships (well, perhaps, if we get a little obsessive about it). This chapter is by no means an attempt at type counselling, but it gives advice on what to look for and what to avoid!

3.1
General types

Fig 3.1: Centro Sans
Centro Sans by Panos Vassiliou provides the typographer with a robust text type that has plenty of charter in heavier weights at display sizes.

Fig 3.2: Arabic text types
This example shows a detail of Arabic text types designed and produced by Boutros Arabic Typography, London.

Text types

Text typefaces are designed to be set at relatively small sizes to allow for continuous reading. These are generally designed in such a way that they are perhaps not immediately obvious or recognizable in context; they work best when they let us get on with the job of reading, without impeding our ability to do so. The best typefaces enable a pleasurable reading experience; the text appears even and grey in colour as type texture and allows for the smooth flow of reading. Letterforms are clear and legible and, within words and paragraphs, no one letterform particularly dominates or stands out from the rest.

Text types are the workhorses of typography, they are the most ubiquitous of types, yet the least recognized or distinguishable to the general reader. Ordinariness is a vital feature of successful text types. The types themselves may be beautiful on close inspection, but when set for lengthy tracts of text matter, it is their inert qualities – when composed together – that belies their strength and ingenuity.

The earliest typography required text type to be acceptable to readers, with qualities similar to various forms of handwriting. Many of these early typefaces survive today as revivals or modern interpretations of classical models. The more modern sans serif types work equally well as text types and display types. The majority of text types, however, still owe much to the archetypes of the fifteenth century, the quality and clarity of which look surprisingly modern today.

Fig 3.1

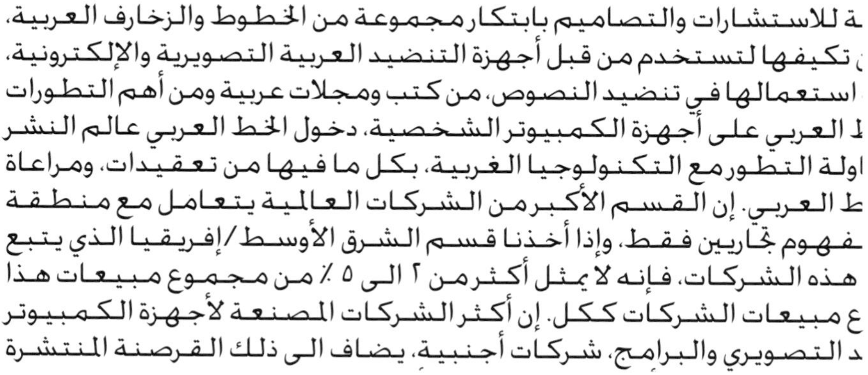

ـة للاستشارات والتصاميم بابتكار مجموعة من الخطوط والزخارف العربية،
، تكيفها لتستخدم من قبل أجهزة التنضيد العربية التصويرية والإلكترونية،
استعمالها في تنضيد النصوص، من كتب ومجلات عربية ومن أهم التطورات
لـ العربي على أجهزة الكمبيوتر الشخصية، دخول الخط العربي عالم النشر
اولة التطور مع التكنولوجيا الغربية، بكل ما فيها من تعقيدات، ومراعاة
ط العربي. إن القسم الأكبر من الشركات العالمية يتعامل مع منطقة
فهوم جتاريين فقط. وإذا أخذنا قسم الشرق الأوسط/إفريقيا الذي يتبع
هذه الشركات، فإنه لا يمثل أكثر من ٢ الى ٥ ٪ من مجموع مبيعات هذا
ع مبيعات الشركات ككل. إن أكثر الشركات المصنعة لأجهزة الكمبيوتر
د التصويري والبرامج، شركات أجنبية، يضاف الى ذلك القرصنة المنتشرة

Fig 3.2

Fig 3.3

Caslon Pro
Minion Pro
Bembo
Ehrhardt
Garamond Pr
Plantin
Baskerville

Pro an libris appetere reprehendunt, no illum essent eruditi vix, primis epicuri ne qui. Ad pro cibo malorum scribentur. Has in ridens temporibus comprehensam, tantas docendi eligendi mel ex. Ut ludus zril sea, pro essent causae te. Eam mundi dolore an, case equidem moderatius nec ei.
Ehrhardt 11/13.5pt

Pro an libris appetere reprehendunt, no illum essent eruditi vix, primis epicuri ne qui. Ad pro cibo malorum scribentur. Has in ridens temporibus comprehensam, tantas docendi eligendi mel ex. Ut ludus zril sea, pro essent causae te. Eam mundi dolore an, case equidem moderatius nec ei.
Bell 11/13.5pt

Pro an libris appetere reprehendunt, no illum essent eruditi vix, primis epicuri ne qui. Ad pro cibo malorum scribentur. Has in ridens temporibus comprehensam, tantas docendi eligendi mel ex. Ut ludus zril sea, pro essent causae te. Eam mundi dolore an, case equidem moderatius nec ei.
Bodoni 11/13.5pt

Fig 3.4

Fig 3.3: Classic text types
Studying some of the classic text types helps develop an awareness and appreciation of their subtleties of form. At first glance these can look very similar, to the untrained eye. However, there are certainly constraints to which successful text type forms must adhere.

Fig 3.4: Type 'colour'
The subtle variations in the forms of text types can be seen most apparently in the 'colour' or 'texture' of the type when set at reading sizes.

Fig 3.5

Fig 3.5: Big is beautiful
A beautiful example of
a nineteenth-century
display fat face italic,
issued by Caslon c.1821.

Display types

Display types are in complete contrast to text types in terms of their function and use. It is the job of a display type to stand out, to be expressive, to make a statement rather than to blend in. Display type is a more recent phenomenon than one might expect.

The development of the Industrial Revolution saw the emergence of display types in the UK. Thanks to the machine age and the introduction of Koenig's 1814 steam-powered printing press, mass production came to influence the shape of typography. The ability to produce more and print quickly meant that advertisers could seize the new technology and use it to their advantage. With this came the need to stand out from the crowd.

The first display faces appear as variations or even aberrations of the Modern or Didone book text types from the turn of the nineteenth century. Although a few decorated or ornamented types existed before this period, it is really the development of the Moderns, which became bigger and fatter in terms of stroke width, contrast and variation, that we associate with the first display types.

Type founder Robert Thorne is often credited as producing the first display type with the invention of the fat face. However, there is little evidence to substantiate this and its tentative early development can be traced back to types produced by William Cottrell, to whom Thorne had once served as an apprentice.

After Thorne's death in 1820 his type foundry was sold to William Thorowgood; it was then that the first printed specimens of fat face and Egyptian types appeared. The first slab serifs and sans serifs were given the title Egyptians due to contemporary tastes and fashions for the unusual and exotic, rather than any true influence of Middle Eastern aesthetic.

Fiona Ross and non-Latin types

Dr Fiona Ross's career in non-Latin type design and typography stems from her PhD studies in Indian paleography and earlier postgraduate studies in Sanskrit and Pali. From 1978 to 1989 she worked for Linotype (UK) and was responsible for the design of their non-Latin fonts and typesetting schemes. She followed Walter Tracy to become the company's manager, also the first woman to manage the company.

Along with Mike Fellows, she developed phonetic keyboard schemes for Indian scripts that were adopted by the main newspaper publishers in India in the 1980s. It was a major achievement that paved the way for the development of desktop publishing within the Indian subcontinent.

Her work has included consultancy for companies such as Adobe, Apple, Linotype, Monotype and the Open University, amongst others. She has designed over 12 Indian script typefaces for Linotype alone, including the well-known Linotype Bengali with fellow type designer Tim Holloway.

Ross has received widespread recognition for her non-Latin type design work within the typographic community. Her awards include Type Directors Club Awards in 2006 for Adobe Arabic and 2008 for Adobe Thai and Vodafone Hindi.

Today Fiona is Reader in Non-Latin Type Design & Curator of the Non-Latin Type Collection, she also lectures in non-Latin typeface design on the Typeface Design MA at Reading University's Department of Typography and Graphic Communication. She is the author of numerous articles and books on non-Latin typeface design and theory, including *The Printed Bengali Character and its Evolution* (1999) revised (2009).

Fig 3.6:
Non-Latin types
Examples of Fiona
Ross's work shown here
are: Linotype Bengali
in red (including detail
of a single character)
and Adobe Devanagari,
shown in black. Both
scripts translate as:
'typographic design'
in Bengali and Hindi
respectively.

Linotype Bengali
typeface designed for
newspaper Ananda
Bazar Patrika (in daily
use since 1982).

Designers: Tim Holloway
and Fiona Ross for
Linotype Limited Year of
initial design: 1978/79;
Year of publication: by
Linotype Limited (UK)
1980

Adobe Devanagari
commissioned by
Adobe Inc for use for
screen and print.

Designers: Tim Holloway
and Fiona Ross with
Tiro Typeworks Year of
design: 2005: Year of
publication: by Adobe
Inc. 2009; Year of
release: 2011

Fig 3.6

Harmonious types

Most well-designed types provide a harmonious set of variants to work with. If we use one typeface or one family of types, the chances are that these are going to work well together. Indeed, there are now many super families, which provide a ready-mixed selection of serif, sans serif and slab serif, and we don't necessarily need to worry about what to mix and match to get the balance right. It's a different case, however, when we select two or more typefaces that may not be related or part of a super family. This is when it is essential to develop an 'eye'.

There are some factors that can help in creating a harmonious balance between unrelated types. A good sense of the history of typeface development is useful and it should be part of the designer's remit. However, simply taking the time to study how typefaces really look in respect to one another – working out what visual cues or semiotic values are embodied within the type design – can take us a long way in making decisions about what works best. For example, if we selected Garamond as a text typeface and wanted a sans serif type to work alongside it for headings, Gill Sans or Helvetica would work harmoniously in terms of relationship, possibly because they both have some form of human quality in the way they are drawn. However, Futura or Bauhaus would appear awkward or wrong, perhaps because they are more geometric in appearance.

We seem to respond to typographic contrast – it gives us clear distinction in terms of hierarchy. The balance needs to be subtle, however, otherwise it would be like sitting two awkward guests together at a dinner party. They might be interesting individuals, but they are not going to get along!

Fig 3.7

Fig 3.8

خط Palatino Arabic من تصميم ندين شاهين والأستاذ هيرمن زايف. صُمم هذا الخط على أصول خط النسخ ولكنه يمزج بعض المواصفات والميزات من خط الثلث. وخُصص خط بالاتينو العربي للاستخدام في طباعة الكتب. يتميز التصميم بأناقة وانسجام احرفه مما يخوله خطاً مناسباً للاستعمال في الاحجام الكبيرة. يمكن الحصول على خط بالاتينو العربي من خلال Linotype ويحتوي على الاحرف اللاتينية من خط Palatino nova .

Fig 3.7: Contrasting types
The harmonious use of types in this example of letterpress printing by Christopher Wakeling is evident, as too is contrast and hierarchy.

Fig 3.8: Palatino Arabic
A collaboration between Lebanese designer Nadine Chahine and Professor Hermann Zapf. Palatino Arabic is based on the Al-Ahram typeface designed by Zapf in 1956 – reworked to complement the Palatino Nova family.

Fig 3.9: Great Ideas
Catherine Dixon's
cover design as part
of Penguin's Great
Ideas series, celebrates
the cacophony of
types found within
Victorian posters, whilst
referencing the street
slang of the period, a
theme within the book's
content.

Contrasting types

Selecting typefaces for a project can often be one of the most difficult decisions to make, especially for novice designers. You will have heard time and time again the adage 'keep it simple'. It can be applied to many areas and contexts regarding design, including type and typography.

Make small steps as you develop your design palette. If you can't stick to one typeface for the task at hand, make it two; there are few instances where you should need to use any more than this (although some complicated typographic work may require one or two more).

You can create contrast with just one type family. For example, light, bold and the type's associated variants can be chosen to contrast against each other. This is also useful in order to establish hierarchy between text and headings if required.

If you need to use two typefaces, make sure you establish a good, clear contrast between the types. For example, you may want to use a classic text typeface, such as Garamond, for body copy and contrast this with a bold sans serif, such as Akzidenz Grotesk, for headings or subheadings. Using too many types creates confusion; equally, the use of similar or low contrast types can look like a mistake. For example, if you selected Gill Sans for your text type and Futura for headings and subheadings, they would look too closely related.

Type choice can create the voice of a design; too many voices create a cacophony. Try to avoid making those voices that are heard talk at the same level, otherwise it will be difficult to make a distinction between them.

Fig 3.9

Awkward types

There are several ways in which types can appear awkward in terms of their application to typography. One of these is appropriateness, or rather inappropriateness, where strange choices of typeface for a given context can appear awkward or just wrong. For example, the use of Comic Sans for warning signs would be (and is) unacceptable. It is important to evaluate the semiotic values a typeface may communicate rather than making selections based upon personal taste alone. The same goes for mixing types within typographic work. We mentioned briefly that contrast is an important consideration when using two typefaces together, but if that contrast is taken to extremes – for example, using Centaur with Comic Sans – that would just be plain wrong!

Depending on the context, most applications of type need some thorough and robust testing before committing to use. Display types won't work for text and, whereas you can generally use text types for display, they tend to look rather heavy at display and titling sizes. Their characters can look too wide, as can their spacing. Serifs often look too large and heavy at display sizes. Yet some of the visual attributes of text types can provide for some pleasant surprises when scaled very large, particularly in some types where the smallest optically drawn sizes (such as 6pt) are used.

In principle, however, select and use types as they were intended. Most typefaces take a long time to design and develop and their intended use is often part of that development. Take some time to research a little more about the typeface you select for the next project or job you work on.

ᴗᴗᴋᴇᴧᴧ

ɔPQRS

ᴜᴊVWXY

ɜ4567

Fig 3.10

Fig 3.10: Not so awkward now
Paul Renner's first designs for Futura contained some very unusual and awkward characters that never made the final version released by the Bauer Type Foundry in 1927.

These examples are courtesy of Neufville Digital.

Futura ND released by Neufville Digital, a joint-venture of Visualogik and Bauer Types, successor of the Bauersche Giesserei.

Legibility

The terms legibility and readability are often used in reference to the selection of types and their appropriateness within typographic work. They are regarded as cornerstones, particularly of text type designs and their use in typographic matter. They are, however, not to be confused as the same thing.

Legibility simply refers to the qualities that are discernible to the eye; the clarity of type or type matter. For example, ensuring that a capital B is clearly so and not a number 8.

Typeface designers work hard to ensure that the individual glyphs within a typeface design adhere to expectations and represent identifiable characters for reading. The legibility of a typeface, then, is inherent within the design of the type. It includes characteristics such as stroke modulation (the changes from thick to thin); relationships between proportions of character width and height; x-height to ascender and descender relationships; serif size and formation; the relationship between the shapes of individual characters; the size and shape of counters; diacritical marks and punctuation.

All of these relationships affect the legibility of type. It is when the type is formed into words and paragraphs that both legibility and readability can become an issue.

Facete consetetur ei mea, ne vix vero antiopam complectitur, solet suavitate sed ea. Ea harum dolore iracundia vix, ex discere insolens vim, ea suas altera nam! Stet doctus mei cu. Ut nec semper quaestio suscipiantur.

Id mutat interesset scribentur his, ea summo appareat mediocritatem eos, vim ut erant possim. Nisl explicari ut usu. Eleifend omittantur in vim, eam ne clita prodesset repudiandae. Qui ne lorem delenit conclusionemque, quot simul ponderum vis ne. In mea inani torquatos, brute animal et sea, labore necessitatibus an sed. Sed magna oporteat instructior et, usu ex audire vulputate?

Inani denique ei nec, populo veritus sit in. No usu dicunt fuisset, ius graece definiebas ei. Vis eruditi maluisset ut, velit aperiam iracundia cu per. Ne quis facer mea. Malorum scribentur id sit, sea postea doming dolores ex. Ei vel labitur dolores, suas sale pri no.

Facete consetetur ei mea, ne vix vero antiopam complectitur, solet suavitate sed ea. Ea harum dolore iracundia vix, ex discere insolens vim, ea suas altera nam! Stet doctus mei cu. Ut nec semper quaestio suscipiantur.

Id mutat interesset scribentur his, ea summo appareat mediocritatem eos, vim ut erant possim. Nisl explicari ut usu. Eleifend omittantur in vim, eam ne clita prodesset repudiandae. Qui ne lorem delenit conclusionemque, quot simul ponderum vis ne. In mea inani torquatos, brute animal et sea, labore necessitatibus an sed. Sed magna.

Fig 3.12

Fig 3.12: Legibility
A problem when display types are selected for use at text sizes is that their forms are less legible when reduced.

3.4
Seeing is believing

Readability

There have been many studies of readability and legibility in relation to typography and wider studies of language and psychology. Various studies have been conducted in relation to reading and perception, which include speed of reading; distance reading; peripheral vision and reading; eye movements and fatigue.

In relation to design and typography, it is useful to have knowledge of some of the well-known studies, but this is something that will come with time and further immersion in the subject.

The selection of types should involve careful consideration of the following: how will the type be used and in what context? Who are the audience and where will the designed work be seen or read?

Readability, then, is enabled by the appropriate selection of types. In a typographic context it is affected by the following: point size; line length; letter spacing; word spacing; line spacing (or leading); kerning and tracking, and hyphenation and justification.

Typeface designers design and test their types to work within the constraints and conventions of appropriateness. They have no control, however, over the use of their types by the graphic designer or typographer. Again, this is where the users of type must consider undertaking a little research and testing of their own to ensure that types selected are fit for purpose. It is one thing to choose a legible type, but will it appear readable in context?

Fig 3.13

Selecting text typefaces

Text types are by far the most ubiquitous: any text document, be it a book, magazine, newspaper, annual report, web page or any other designed artefact that contains large amounts of text intended for continuous reading, must employ a good text typeface.

It is the designer's duty, when choosing the text type, to consider whether the text will be read at length. The reading experience should be considered as being paramount.

Given the mass of typefaces available today it may seem like a difficult job for the novice to choose a good text typeface. How do you decide? What do you look for? Legibility and readability have already been mentioned and these are key attributes to look for in any good text type. When set as continuous text, a good text type will have an even or grey colour or texture. Most good text types won't vary towards extremes in any way, the width of characters appear as gentle transitions in respect to one another.

Look for an even width-to-height ratio in the characters: not too skinny or too wide. The x-height of the type is also important to consider. Choose a type that has a good x-height, which is neither too large nor too small. The relationship of x-height to ascender height and descender depth should appear balanced.

Be careful of choosing types that have very large counters: in continuous text these can look like holes in the type colour/texture. The stroke widths of the characters should look regular; transitions from thick to thin parts of the strokes should be even and gentle, not harsh or abrupt. Types that have very quirky or odd characters should also be avoided: these cause spots or patches within the text. Finally, avoid types with too many ligatures; these too can create hotspots in the text, which, at best, become tiring to read.

Fig 3.14

**Fig 3.14: Text type –
large and small**
A good text type should
be able to be set at
text as well as display
sizes, although specialist
titling variants are
preferable where they
exist for the latter.

Delenit fuisset referentur ex per, no solum aliquid mentitum nam. Cum mucius suscipit petentium cu, an vel odio atomorum, vocent viderer vel ex. Ad veniam pericula pri? Ei sonet facilisis sea, ei mel eros eirmod, stet tibique ne duo.

Caslon

Bembo

Fig 3.15

1

Fig 3.16

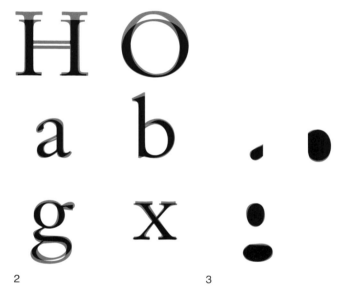

Lorem ipsum dolor sit amet, usu sumo munere ei, pro ea probo malorum perfecto, nam ea munere scripta definitionem. Error dolor ex sit, ea eam admodum commune. Ullum persius neglegentur in vim. An brute voluptatibus vix, ex vel odio indoctum democritum. Ea mei suavitate maluisset, vis porro solet munere at.

Lorem ipsum dolor sit amet, usu sumo munere ei, pro ea probo malorum perfecto, nam ea munere scripta definitionem. Error dolor ex sit, ea eam admodum commune. Ullum persius neglegentur in vim. An brute voluptatibus vix, ex vel odio indoctum democritum. Ea mei suavitate maluisset, vis porro solet munere at.

2   3

Fig 3.15: Caslon vs. Bembo
In terms of the form and width and height of the character settings, you can see how closely both Caslon (red) and Bembo (cyan) perform.

Fig 3.16: X-heights
Closer inspection reveals that part of their success as good text types is that they share similar 'x-heights'. The width of the characters and internal counter shapes are also of very similar proportions. These are essential attributes for a type to work well at small sizes.

Fig 3.17

Selecting display typefaces

In contrast to text types, when using display types, almost anything goes. The choice of any type, be it text or display, will affect the overall look and feel of a design, but it is through the use of display types that typography is most often seen.

It may well be the case that the type being used for text is the same type used for display. Most of the time this is fine. However, it should be remembered that many text types have accompanying display or titling versions that are specifically designed for use at large sizes.

In general, display types provide the more obvious typographic image within many designs. The hallmarks of a good text typeface design need not apply to display typefaces at all. It is really a case of selecting a display type that sits comfortably with the text types and that is appropriate for the job.

There are many display typefaces of the nineteenth century that were considered atrocious in their day and are now celebrated for the very nature of their unusual or bizarre appearance. Similarly, the late 1980s and early 1990s saw an exploration of the digital age through the release of many unusual and challenging display types. Many of these may be seen as naive or just plain ugly today, but some will survive the vagaries of time and fashion, much like their nineteenth-century counterparts have done.

Working with display types really offers the chance to play. Make it big, make it bold, make it beautiful: display types are not for the fainthearted, they are the exhibitionists of the typographic world and demand their place in the spotlight.

Fig 3.17: Making a statement
Display types usually want to be seen! This poster design by the author also includes bespoke typefaces designed by him. The numerals become more than just type, forming the ground and colour-fields for the text to sit upon.

Appropriateness

The choice of typeface for a project not only enables the legibility and readability of a text, but it can also act as the voice of the design. It can lend gravitas where needed or provide light relief from the everyday or humdrum. The correct choice of type can breathe life into a design or, conversely, it can make the reading experience awkward or dull.

Knowing how to choose good or appropriate typefaces can often be problematic for beginners. It is something that takes time to acquire a feel for. It's really a case of immersing yourself in the activity and training the eye.

Task

Find three examples of design in which you feel the choice of typeface has been well considered and is appropriate in relation to the overall design and content. Mark up what works and why. Can you identify the typefaces being used? Has consideration been given to the size of the typeface? Have the typefaces been used correctly or appropriately in terms of text or display settings?

Once you have identified these examples, repeat the exercise with three examples that you feel have not worked successfully. Ask the same questions to consider why this might be the case.

Tip

It may be worth beginning with designs that you know others have remarked upon as having merit or being noteworthy. What do others see in these? Do you agree with them?

Fig 3.18

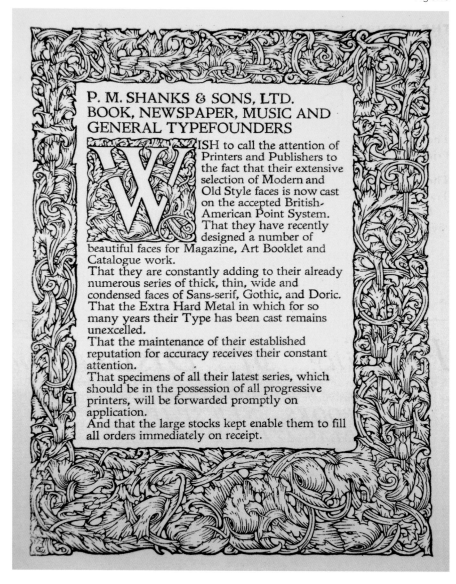

Chapter 4
Old, new and familiar faces

More often than not we use metaphor and simile to describe type. More often still, we relate to our own human traits, personalities and experiences when describing type. Just like any other visual stimuli, types have their unique forms; forms that carry semiotic value.

We read language set in type, but we also read the form of type, from the individual character to the texture created by the paragraph; we interpret its visual appearance as well as its functional characteristics. Traces of lineage and even genealogy can also be found in the design of types. We can see the relationships between typefaces and groups of types.

It's important for designers to know how these are related in order to make an informed decision, rather than one based on the way type looks. Often however, it's the place we have to start. This chapter looks at the ways in which we might initially describe type to further develop our understanding.

Fashionable types

As in any other walk of life, type and typography are subject to passing fashions and trends. The problem with most fashions and trends, however, is that they don't last very long. Just like clothes, typefaces can appear trendy and current, only to look jaded months later. Some manage to escape the trendy trap and appear perennially cool. Others that go out of fashion may return, often slightly updated to fit with the mood of the times.

Fashionable types can be great fun and make your work look really up to date – which is great. How many times, though, have you bought an item of clothing only to wear it once? Selecting type can be a bit like this, too. Quirky type normally calls for quirky applications, so use it sparingly. Some designers are able to create beautiful, fashionable work using only a very limited range of fonts.

Some areas of visual culture, such as fashion magazine design, have made certain types de rigueur. Mastheads set in condensed Moderns, with high contrast thick and thin strokes, have become synonymous with fashion publications. It's interesting to note that the typefaces cut by Firmin Didot and Giambattista Bodoni as book typefaces in the late 1700s (or at least their influences) are seen as the accepted height of typographic fashion today.

Fig 4.1: Carousel
NB Studio's Casa Décor identity makes use of the typeface Carousel, a Modern packed full of character.

Fig 4.2: Vogue Italia
Literally a fashionable type, these Bodoni and Didot forms have adorned the front covers of many of the world's most high-profile fashion magazines.

Fig 4.1

Fig 4.2

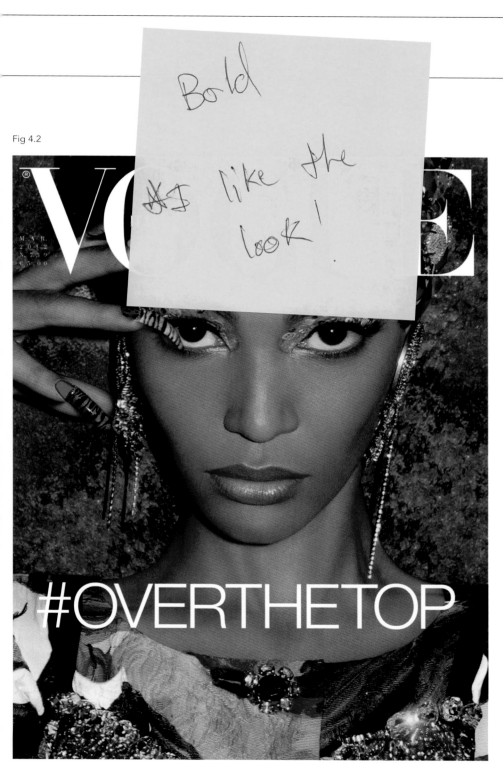

Fig 4.3

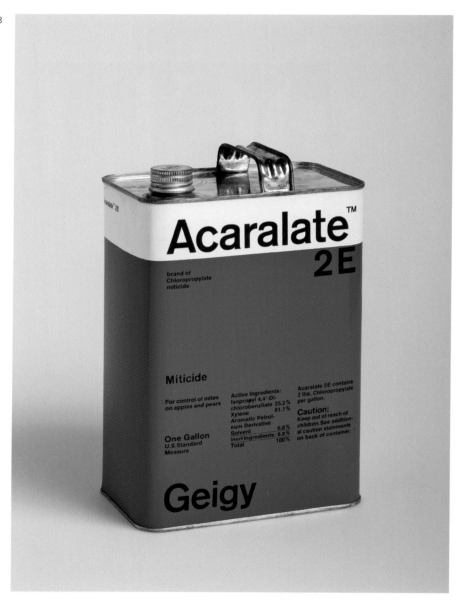

Ubiquitous types

Just as there are some typefaces that are cult perennials in that they seem to be constantly fashionable, there are others that seem to be used by everyone, everywhere, often with complete disregard as to whether they are fashionable or not. You don't need a background in graphic design and typography to have knowledge of them – most people see them every day. Typefaces such as Helvetica are so commonly used, and found in so many different applications, that they have become equally venerated and vilified by members of the design community.

We have become so used to seeing Verdana on web pages that we become less appreciative of the fact that it was designed by Matthew Carter specifically to improve the on-screen reading experience. Arial and Times New Roman have also suffered from overexposure and come in for much criticism from designers at times. And of course, Comic Sans cannot go without a mention here. Another victim of its own success, it has certainly found many applications for which it was never intended.

One of the problems with such typefaces is that they tend to get used, by designers and non-designers alike, as default types. They are chosen because they are the default types within software packages or because there has been little thought or consideration given to the type selection.

Just as with fashionable typefaces, we can tire of seeing these ubiquitous types. Used correctly, they can work well. They can also be interpreted as a lazy choice, however. If we are not careful, all too often the 'system' fonts can seem to dictate design choice, resulting in unimaginative design.

Fig 4.3:
Akzidenz Grotesk
Although first developed at the end of the nineteenth century, Akzidenz Grotesk became a worldwide superstar in terms of sans serif designs. The forerunner to Helvetica, it still looks fresh today. Here, Geigy's corporate style is implemented in this 1967 canister design by Markus Löw.

Delicate types

Delicate types with very thin strokes and flowing lines can add an air of sophistication to design projects. Sans serif and slab serif ultra-thin types can look cool and elegant whilst retaining a sense of modernity. Technology today allows the design and print of ultra-light characters that would previously have been difficult to manufacture and print from.

Likewise, there are many typefaces that were designed with thin strokes and delicate details for printing in metal types. These types would have pressed firmly on the surface of the paper, creating 'ink-squash' or spread, making very fine details slightly stronger when printed. Much of the fine detailing of such types was translated in the design of early digital versions. However, because they would not be printed in the same manner, much of that detailing could appear too thin when produced with modern printing machines and processes.

Many very light typefaces need special consideration for use in practice. For example, if used too small, details may begin to disappear in print and on screen. Very thin typefaces or types with very fine details can also be problematic when reversed out from blocks of colour, especially those made up from the CMYK process. Script types, particularly those based upon copperplate or running-hand forms, may need their entry and exit strokes to be joined so as to avoid broken and disruptive patterns. The lavish swash capitals that can accompany such fonts are not intended to sit together, so they should be used in a combination of upper and lower case.

Fig 4.4: Scripts
Scripts such as Matthew Carter's Snell Roundhand, are designed to be used in a 'running-hand' style – as joined upper and lower case (top). The setting of all capitals in this sort of type (below) is to be avoided.

Fig 4.5: Archer Hairline
Types such as Archer Hairline, by Hoefler & Frere-Jones, require some care in use due to the very fine stroke weight.

Fig 4.4

Fig 4.5

Classic types

What makes a typeface a classic? In most cases, it is those that stand the test of time. Many typefaces that appear to have staying power eventually become regarded as classics. What it is about them that gives them this staying power, though?

There are certain traits that any good typeface must display:

- Good proportions of x-height to ascender and descender height and depth;
- Character widths that aren't too narrow or wide;
- Well-proportioned, open counters and in most cases no dramatic changes in contrast or modulation between thick and thin strokes.

There are other factors, however, that can determine whether or not a typeface becomes a classic, such as whether or not the design or style of that type created a paradigm shift in the way type was conceived or perceived. Some types exemplify certain traditions, such as handwriting and lettering. Type that constitutes a classification should also be considered a classic. For example, Akzidenz Grotesk can be considered a classic sans serif, Garamond a classic old face.

Classic status may also result from associated use of type. After all, a typeface is useless if it never finds an application. In Darwinian terms, in time only the fittest survive – this is perhaps the best indicator of a true classic.

'From all these experiences the most important thing I have learned is that legibility and beauty stand close together and that type design, in its restraint, should be only felt but not perceived by the reader.'

Adrian Frutiger

Akzidenz Grotesk	Albertus	Baskerville
Bodoni	Caslon	Centaur
Clarendon	Ehrhardt	**Franklin Gothic**
Futura	Garamond	Gill Sans
Grotesque	Helvetica	Meta
Optima	Plantin	**Rockwell**
Times	Univers	Verdana

Fig 4.6

Minion Pro

Regular

Italic

Medium

Medium Italic

Semibold

Semibold Italic

Bold

Bold Italic

Bold Condensed

Bold Condensed Italic

Fig 4.7

Fig 4.7 Minion Pro
There are classics and there are workhorses. Robert Slimbach's Minion Pro may well appear fairly ubiquitous, but its family of variants, expert characters and language coverage make for a very resilient type.

Real workhorses

For any novice or aspiring designer, it is important to be able to select types that are not just appropriate in a conceptual sense, but also get the job done: that they are going to work well at text or display sizes; that they are going to set and print well or display well on digital devices. Many of the classic type attributes, just discussed, translate to those types we might consider 'workhorses'. These types are robust and can withstand use in many applications, whether in lengthy text settings or high street signage.

Many day-to-day pieces of printed ephemera require workhorse types. Newspapers, books, magazines, web pages and wayfinding schemes all require types that will 'do the job' time and again. Garamond has been around in various guises since the late fifteenth century and it is still going strong; it has perhaps even improved with age in many respects. Verdana, designed by Matthew Carter and released in 1996, is arguably the world's most readable on-screen typeface, and in this sense it is a true workhorse for the digital generation. Its ubiquity and purpose as an on-screen type, however, means that its use in print is less favourably perceived by graphic designers and typographers. The ever-present Helvetica can be considered a classic as well as a workhorse and, despite its detractors, is one of the few typefaces that can be used in virtually any design application from web pages to signage systems.

'Minion Pro is inspired by classical, old style typefaces of the late Renaissance, a period of elegant and highly readable type designs. It combines the aesthetic and functional qualities that make text type highly readable for computerized typesetting needs.'

scholarlytype.com

Originals

It is fair to say that many new typefaces today are originals, in that they have been produced for the first time as digital types. Whether their designs are truly original or not is a different story. It has already been mentioned that some typefaces are based on earlier models, such as Bembo, which was based on Francesco Griffo's fifteenth-century types for *De Aetna*. An original typeface can change the way we think about how type has been, or should be, designed; originals will essentially add something new. In this sense, we can see that Bembo can be regarded as a revival of Griffo's type; Griffo's version is original, in that it became a model type for others to follow. It set a standard that had previously not been achieved in the design of types.

Today, truly original types are much harder to find but there are some, such as Jeremy Tankard's Fenland typeface, which explores the internal relationships of form between the letterforms, and how these are generated. Much of the explosion of experimentation of digital typeface design belongs to the late 1980s through to the late 1990s. The epochal shift from physical technologies (metal type, wood type and phototype) to digital technologies brought with it a new wave of designers who wanted to respond to the possibilities of the digital age. Although there were many interesting typefaces produced during this time, very few remain useful or interesting to us today. Most original typefaces today still follow some form of historical precedent in their influence or forms, derived from the marks of tool incidence such as the pen, brush or chisel.

Fig 4.8

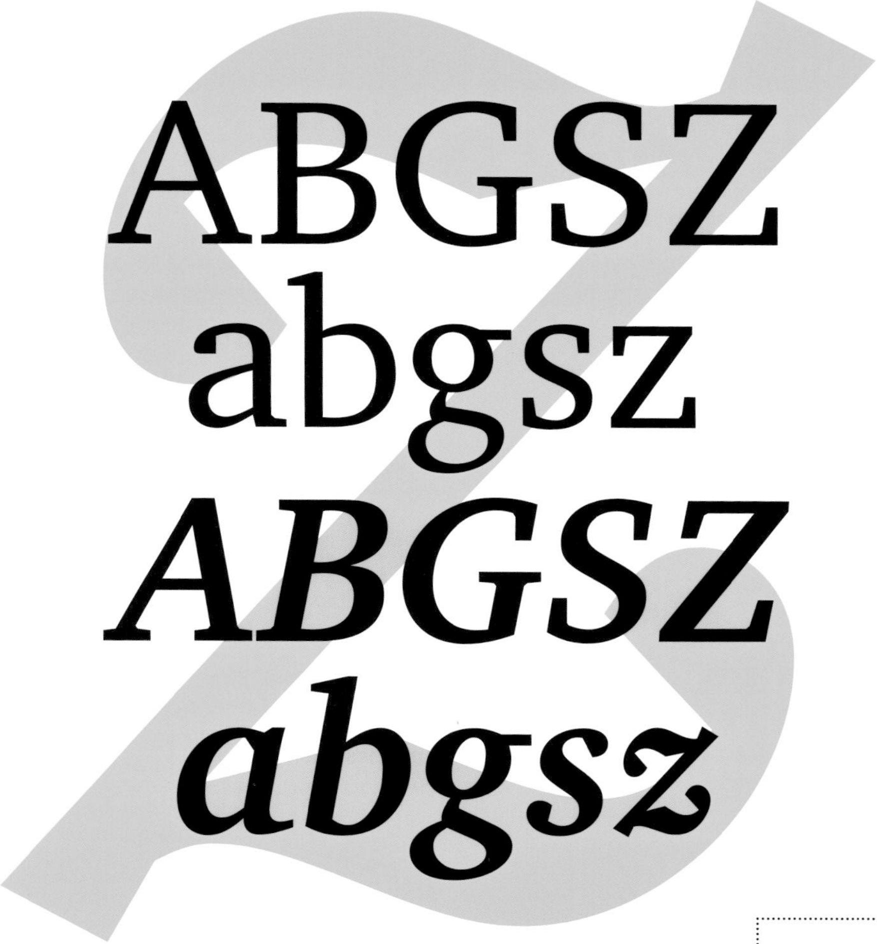

ABGSZ
abgsz
ABGSZ
abgsz

Fig 4.8: A true original
Matthew Carter sought to solve the problems of computer storage file-size in developing this serif typeface. Because the design used fewer curves than a conventional serif type, Carter was able to reduce the overall file size. Technology has a habit of progressing however, and the size of font files no longer poses a problem.

The Garamonds

The previous sections have covered fashion, ubiquity, delicacy, classic status, workhorse strength, originality and revivalism. Garamond is a typeface that could be said to fit in to all of these categories. There is, in fact, no one real Garamond typeface, but many types that are interpretations of Claude Garamond's original types. These belong to the category Garalde, or old face, and although they may look similar, on closer inspection they are quite different. The differences in appearance of the available Garamond types today are partly due to historical misattribution.

Garamond's types were produced in the sixteenth century. They were influenced by the fifteenth-century work of Francesco Griffo, but gained recognition in their own right when they began to appear in the publications of Parisian scholar-printer Robert Estienne. The harmonious relationships of form within Garamond's types contributed to what is considered today as the golden age of French typography.

Confusion for the revivalists and historians was caused by two episodes after Garamond's death in 1561. First, Garamond's punches and matrices were sold to the Antwerp-based printer Christopher Plantin. Punch-cutter Jacques Sabon aquired them and they subsequently appeared in a type specimen issued by the Egenolff-Berner foundry. This specimen provided inspiration for many of the Garamond revivals; it also included italic types cut by Robert Granjon that appeared with Garamond's roman types.

Then, in the seventeenth century, French printer Jean Jannon produced a typeface with very similar characteristics to Garamond's types, which was confiscated by the French royal printing office. In 1825 they were rediscovered and mistakenly attributed to Garamond. Although these mistakes were uncovered in 1927 by typographic historian Beatrice Warde, revivals based on the work of Jannon and the italics of Granjon still bear the Garamond name.

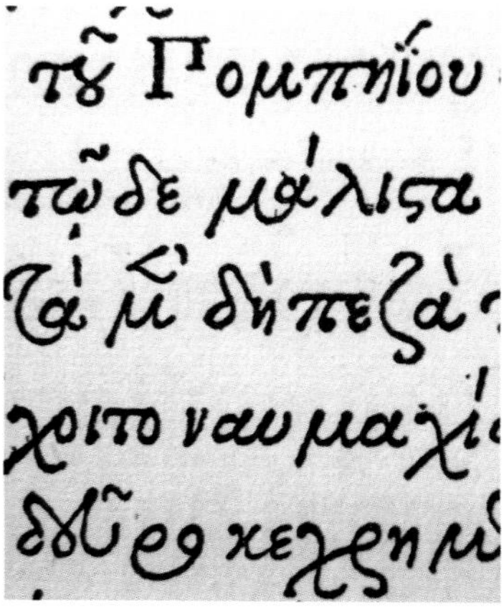

Fig 4.11

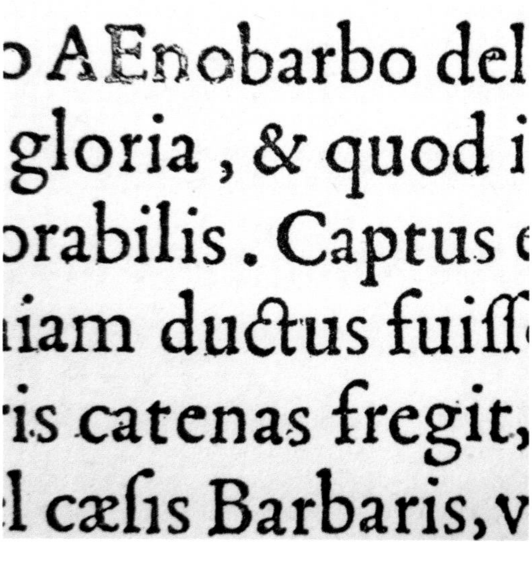

Fig 4.12

Fig 4.11: Grecs du Roi
A sample of Garamond's Greek types used by the French printer Robert Estienne. These types were produced by Garamond for King Francis I of France.

Fig 4.12: Garamond roman
This example of roman type was used by Estienne in Paris, in 1549. It is believed to have been produced Claude Garamond.

4.4
Unique types

Exotic types

Sometimes our design sensibilities need to take a holiday from the regular day job. Perhaps this comes in the form of a project we've been set, or a brief for a new client that requires us to stray from our visual culture comfort zone. For example, we may have been asked to design something with an Eastern feel to it, or perhaps it's for a festival of Arabic cinema to be communicated to an English audience.

We might automatically conjure images of visual references that we think represent those countries prior to our research. Similarly, we might be tempted to use typefaces that evoke some of these 'exotic' qualities. It's a good idea to take care in this area. Using available types that are stylized to represent other nations or cultures can be interpreted as cheap and clichéd at best. For example, Latin types that mimic the Chinese style of brush lettering, or those that bastardize the forms of Devanagari (Indic script) to produce Latin forms, may be familiar sights on food packaging, but these ersatz (substituted and inferior) selections of types really lack imagination, not to mention being rather jokey or, worse still, offensive.

Unless you can make an authentic connection to exotic cultures then avoid the faux exotic, unless of course irony is part of the design brief. In which case, there are plenty of bad taste types to select from!

Fig 4.15: Reza Abedini
This poster for a lecture by Reza Abedini on Persian type and typography includes Persian typeforms that need no Westernized pastiches to communicate their identity.

Fig 4.16: Zanzibar
Gábor Kóthay's Zanzibar type captures the feel of the exotic through the expression of the strokes.

Fig 4.15

Fig 4.16

Unusual types

There are some typefaces so unusual that they might find very little use indeed, but that are perfect for that one-off project. This may be typographic work required in advertising or promotional work, for example. It may be that of the hundreds of thousands of regular typefaces available, none quite captures the essence of what it is you are trying to communicate. Then it may be time to look to the weird and wonderful for inspiration. The appetite for this kind of type never seems to abate. Unfortunately (or perhaps fortunately for some), many of these types fall by the wayside over a period of time. It can take some serious digging to find these rare and sometimes beautiful specimens.

The appearance of unusual types often coincides with shifts in technology, allowing new avenues to be explored in technical reproduction. Mechanized punch-cutting, mechanized typesetting, litho-printing, photocomposition and digital technologies have all contributed to designers testing and pushing the boundaries of experimentation and taste. Most unusual typefaces created in the last 20 years or so should be easier to trace because they were produced digitally. However, there are many from bygone eras that languish in the old specimen books awaiting rediscovery.

Finding the right type for very unusual jobs can be quite time consuming. You may even decide that the only solution is to design your own. Websites such as <www.fontifier.com> and <www.fontstruct.com> offer a quick and easy way to produce types for those unusual applications. You may then decide to take type design seriously from there and investigate the use of professional font editing software programs.

'I do not think of type as something that should be readable. It should be beautiful.'

Ed Benguiat

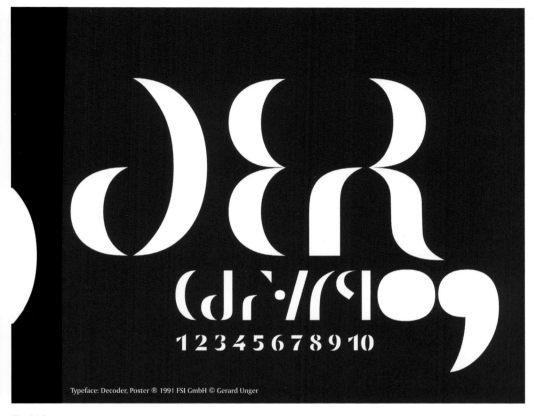

Typeface: Decoder, Poster ® 1991 FSI GmbH © Gerard Unger

Fig 4.18

Fig 4.18: More than the sum of its parts
Gerard Unger's Decoder typeface uses modular forms to create the letterforms. A typeface that is both challenging and intriguing.

Fig 4.19

Future types

Graphic designers often become involved in type design to produce designs that appear to some degree as futuristic, abandoning the handcrafted aesthetic in favour of order, rationalization or modularity. Ultra-modernist designs such as New Alphabet, Gridnik, Fodor, Catalogue and Vormgevers, all designed by Wim Crouwel, have received much acclaim and achieved something of a fetish status among obsessive systems designers. Similar systems in type design can be found in the work of MuirMcNeil's ThreeSix types. Antecedents of these modular forms can be found: a particularly interesting one is Fregio Mecano (circa 1920s), a modular type in which any letterform could be made from a kit of twenty stroke segments.

In truth, however, designers' love of the new and visions of the future when it comes to the possibilities of modular systems, the machine and computer, is nothing new. Rationalist approaches to aligning type and letterforms with geometry and modular systems go back a long way. Sixteenth-century Renaissance writing masters, such as Giambattista Palatino, produced complicated geometric constructions in order to rationalize letterforms, as did the mathematician Fra Luca Pacioli in the construction of his letters for *De Divina Proportione* in 1509.

Grids for letter construction and typeface design also appear in Geoffroy Tory's *Champ Fleury* (1529) and Joseph Moxon's *Mechanick Exercises* (1683). The Romain du Roi (1702), by the French Academy of Sciences, is the earliest form of a grid system, which directly influenced the shaping of the typeface. The punches were cut by Philippe Grandjean, who translated the copperplate engravings of Simonneau. The influence of the Romain du Roi can be found in the types of Pierre Simon Fournier (circa 1742) and John Baskerville (1757), mainly in terms of vertical stress and increased contrast between thick and thin strokes. This goes to prove that experimentation in any era can continue to have an influence long into the future.

Fig 4.19: Modular type
MuirMcNeil's poster for a Wim Crouwel exhibition utilizes their own ThreeSix modular typeface – an homage to the work of Crouwel.

Fig 4.20:
Printed samples
Collecting printed type
specimens, old and
new, is a great way to
appreciate type.

Books and printed samples

It goes without saying that students
should try to consult as many different
books as possible with regard to their
subject, but this also requires a level
of selective reading.

There are many online forums that
can be of great help, but how can
you be sure that you are getting
quality advice? One solution is to
approach these sorts of resources
ready armed. The printed samples and
specimen books of type foundries and
typesetting houses, old and new, are
a great way to begin engaging with
the discipline.

Older specimen books that hold metal
and wood types are especially useful,
as well as being great artefacts to look
through. This is because many of these
firms would have stock of the best
or most useful types for text setting,
knowing that these would be popular
and frequently used. Typesetters knew
the value of quality robust fonts. So
many of these old printed samples and
specimen books are a great way to get
to know some of the classic typefaces.

'Faces of type are like men's faces. They have their own
expression; their complexion and peculiar twists and turns of line
identify them immediately to friends, to whom each is full
of identity.'

J.L. Frazier

Fig 4.20

Fig 4.21

Digital sources

It's fair to say that most typefaces or fonts are sourced online. There are so many typefaces available now that the numbers probably stretch into the hundreds of thousands, making the job of selecting types – particularly good ones – even more difficult now than it ever has been.

The problem with some websites and forums is that there is no real quality control in terms of their opinions and offerings, which is why students need to take in a broad range of sources to ensure that what they are consuming, in communication terms, is healthy and nutritious.

Many students also want to use and download free fonts because they're, well, free. There are some free fonts of worth that are also, importantly, legal to download. Yet there is an ever-increasing number of free fonts, self-published by amateur type designers, which are of very low quality and it is unfortunate to see these being used in student designs. Even reputable digital type foundries may offer selections for fonts by other foundries, from which the quality cannot always be guaranteed. It takes type designers a long time to design and develop a typeface, in some cases many years, so sharing or pirating types is a practice best avoided.

Fig 4.21: FontShop
There are a wide range of quality font suppliers online – FontShop is one of the best known. Students should avoid the low quality free-download sites. Buying fonts may be expensive at times but you can be assured of quality that you won't find on many free font sites.

Old and new

'What goes around comes around' is an old saying that comments on the predictable nature of cyclical patterns in life, be it luck or fashion. Type and typography is also subject to such influences.

Task

Choose a sans serif typeface and a serif typeface from your computer's operating system and use these as a starting point to trace the influences and genetics of each type or style back to an earlier period. Can you find who designed the type? What other types have they designed? Are the types you have chosen originals or revivals? What influenced the design of the types? What was the original date of the design? Was this before digital type existed?

Tip

Begin by trying to work out the type's classification – whether it is a humanist sans or an old face serif, and so on. Then try to find out who designed it. This may give you a clue as to its age. If it's a very old design, how does the digital version differ from the original?

Fig 4.22: Type fashions
Some types may be complete 'one-offs', others more common. They may belong to the same period in terms of origin or influence. Below: An ornamental sixteenth-century decorative capital and an eighteenth-century derived modern – both of Italian extraction.

Fig 4.22

ertain

r, five,

dle,

Chapter 5
Identifying type

Today there are a bewildering number of typefaces available for purchase. Added to this, the Internet has made it possible for those with only a passing interest in designing types to upload, self-publish and share their efforts, in many cases free of charge. This of course gives us a great deal more choice when selecting typefaces; it also makes it much more difficult to determine for certain which typefaces we see around us. This is as true for the professional designer and typographer as it is for the novice or student.

This chapter gives some clues on where to begin when trying to identify types as well as outlining some of the reasons for the difficulties you may encounter when trying to identify the 'face in the crowd'.

Which type is which?

There are thousands of typeface designs available today. There are many more typefaces that are designed solely for use as corporate or proprietary fonts; bespoke designs that are intended to help companies and organizations reinforce a unique identity. It is probably true to say that many modern typefaces are technically better than those designed in the past. Technology has allowed more designers, from many different backgrounds, to become involved in type design at a professional level, whereas only a few years ago this was a preserve of the few.

So then, why do we need new typefaces – aren't there enough already? Such questions have been asked many times but they are ultimately naive. Many designers will argue that they only use a very small number of classic typefaces and that there is no need for any others. This may well be the case, and in some ways this can be a very beneficial and rewarding way to work. However, to decry new design of any nature – be it of typeface, layout, architecture or furniture – is to decry the development of culture and society at any level. Could we really only listen to a handful of songs? Should there only be a limited number of television programmes or movies?

The reason we have so many typefaces is because we can. Some are geared towards a more functional use, such as setting texts, some purely provide aesthetic curiosity, such as display-only settings, and then there is everything else in between. But with so many types, how can we even begin to make sense of them all?

'One of my colleagues is convinced that having a wide range of types to choose from is a complete waste of time. He swears by two typefaces: Gill (1928) and Frutiger (1975), which he uses for road signs (among other things) ... Until 1975, the year in which Adrian Frutiger's eponymous typeface came onto the market, my colleague could only have made half of his selection. It seems to me that this proves the case for continuing to design new typefaces.'

Gerard Unger

Fig 5.1: Familiar faces
Classic text typefaces can look similar. Three of the seven shown here are interpretations of Garamond. Can you identify them?

From top: Apple system Garamond; Adobe Caslon Pro; Minion Pro; Bembo; Stempel Garamond; Ehrhardt MT; Adobe Garamond Pro.

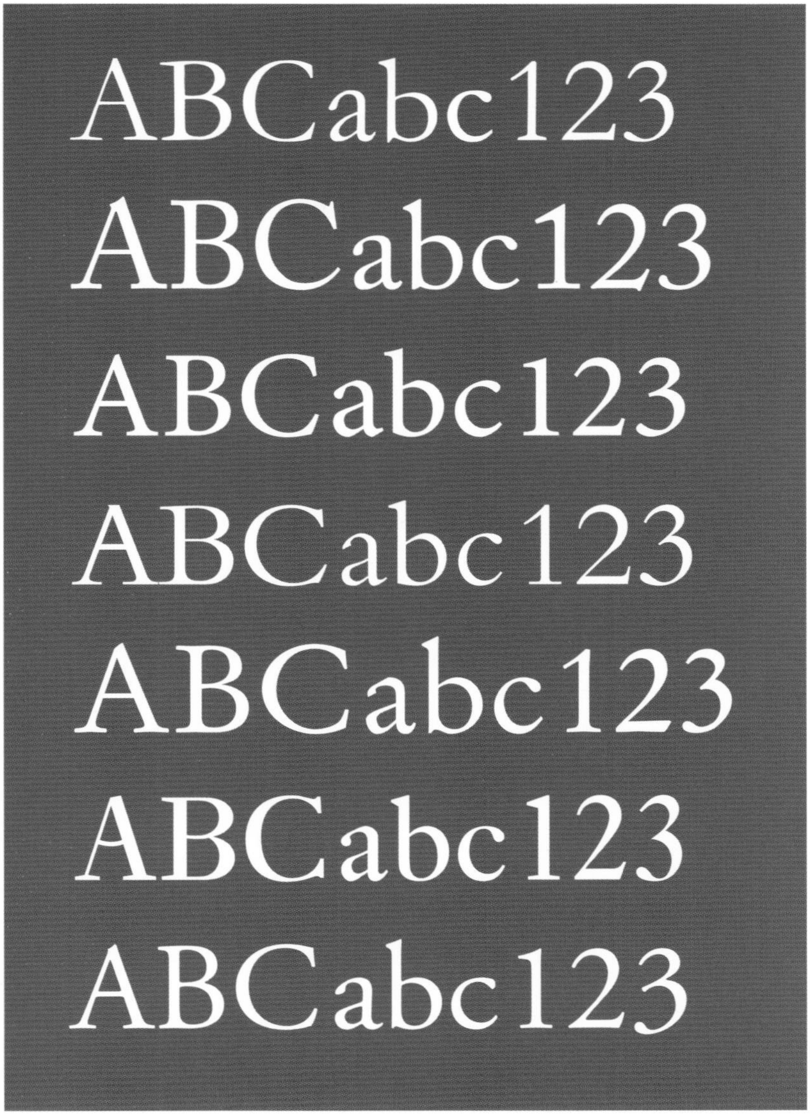

Fig 5.1

Playing the detective

The level at which you are in your design career (or, for those non-designers, the length of time you may have harboured an interest in type) will probably affect how you view or perceive type and what it means to you. You may have an admiration for the classics. Trendy types may be your thing. There may simply be some types that you just like the look of. All of these are, of course, perfectly valid ways of engaging with type, but how do you begin to identify what you are looking at?

Nowadays it is easy to play detective when it comes to identifying types, thanks to online or mobile apps such as 'WhatTheFont'. These allow you to take a picture or a screenshot of a type, submit it through the app and – hey presto! Instant answers, perhaps, but even when such apps return the correct answer, it still doesn't help us develop a sense of what we are looking at.

For this we need to know something of the history of the development of types (a very small amount of which was covered at the beginning of this book). With this history comes the artifice of type: the typefaces themselves, type specimens, the style and aesthetics related to the producers and designers of type, systems of classification, taxonomy and nomenclature. It is useful to develop a broad view of type classification in relation to the historical development of types. This won't tell you everything you need to know and it won't reliably cover every conceivable variation in type design; it will, however, give you a good place to start.

'It would be very unusual to someone to be able to recognize their suit thread by thread – in the same way people don't recognize typefaces letter by letter on the page.'
Matthew Carter

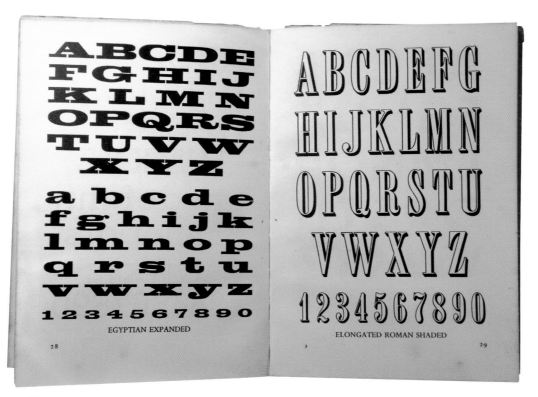

EGYPTIAN EXPANDED

28

ELONGATED ROMAN SHADED

3

29

Fig 5.2

Distinguishing features

A broad classification system such as the Vox-ATypl system mentioned in chapter two (see pages 62–65) is a good framework for gaining familiarity with type history and development and its influences on type design. It is worth noting that this system relates to the identification of typefaces that have developed from a north-west European perspective of type history. The single classification for non-Latins, for example, is hardly sufficient to describe all other type forms that don't find their roots in north-west Europe.

Generally speaking, we tend to see the overall look of a typeface. This is easy to appreciate when we look at a page in a novel, for example. We can begin by focusing on the distinguishing features in the details of the type. For example, is it a serif or sans serif type? If we look at the stress or shading of letters such as the lower case e, c, o or b, d, p, q, is this more upright or diagonal? If the typeface has serifs, what style are they?

Such questions can help us place a typeface within one of the broad categories mentioned previously. From here we can start to look at more specific detail to help us identify the type. Quite often, letters such as the lower case 'a' or 'g' may be good 'spot' letters within a typeface design; the same goes for the upper case 'M' and 'R'. These letters often have details that bring individual or idiosyncratic qualities to a typeface design.

video plagiarius quod vos mos animadverto
video plagiarius quod vos mos animadverto
video plagiarius quod vos mos animadverto
video plagiarius quod vos mos animadverto
video plagiarius quod vos mos animadverto
video plagiarius quod vos mos animadverto
video plagiarius quod vos mos animadverto

Fig 5.3

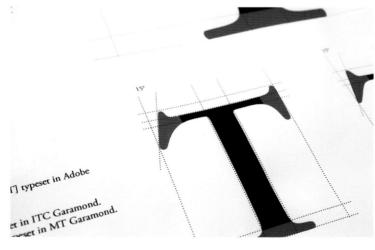

Fig 5.4

Fig 5.3: It's all in the details
Small details in 'signature' letterforms can help in identifying them, along with their general appearance.

Fig 5.4: Under the microscope
Student work by Marie Cleaver. Analysis identifies and distinguishes the properties of different forms of Garamond.

Putting a face to the name

Once you have placed a type design within a broad classification group, identifying and naming the type becomes much easier. You will need reference material, either online or in the form of printed specimen samples, so you can draw comparisons with the design you are trying to identify. You will need to do this at least until you are confident enough to rely on memory or until the overall appearance and details of a type become familiar.

There are so many typefaces based on historical models of type or which reinterpret the past with only a subtle difference in form, that it can be very difficult indeed to name a typeface. The ability to identify types also takes practice, in taking time to look at the details; to marvel at the fact that every little character has been sculpted with care and dedication on the part of the designer. Indeed, it may be necessary to view some contemporary designs from the perspective of those who created them. There may be signature traits in terms of styling and aesthetics that may transcend one design to another when you look at the collective work of a type designer. This helps put a name to the face, and also put a face to the name, quite literally.

'If you remember the shape of your spoon at lunch, it has to be the wrong shape. The spoon and the letter are tools; one to take food from the bowl, the other to take information off the page... When it is a good design, the reader has to feel comfortable because the letter is both banal and beautiful.'

Adrian Frutiger

Fig 5.5

There are two men inside the artist, the poet and the craftsman.

One is born a poet. One becomes a craftsman.

Emile Zola

Fig 5.5: Signature traits
Two types designed by Erik Spiekermann. Top is ITC Officina and below FF Meta. The designer's hand can be seen to influence both sets of forms. Two quite different types that, on close inspection, reveal many similarities.

Erik Spiekermann, a life in type

Erik Spiekermann has had a huge influence on the disciplines of modern type design, typography, graphic design and information design. Born in 1947, he studied History of Art and English at Freie Universität Berlin (Free University Berlin, Germany), funding his studies by running a printing press and setting metal type in the basement of his house.

He set up MetaDesign in 1979 with two other partners after seven years as a freelance designer in London. MetaDesign became Germany's largest design firm with offices in Berlin, London and San Francisco. Meta's clients included Adobe, Apple, Audi, Hewlett Packard, IBM, Nike and Volkswagen.

In 1989 he founded FontShop, the first mail-order distributor of digital fonts. The FontFont range of types are now published by FSI FontShop International.

Spiekermann's early typeface designs were redrawings of older Berthold metal types Berliner Grotesk (1913/1979) and Lo-Type (1914/1980). His other fonts include ITC Officina Sans (1990), ITC Officina Serif (1990), FF Meta (1991–1998), FF Govan (2001), FF Info (2000), FF Unit (2003) and FF Meta Serif (with Christian Schwartz and Kris Sowersby, 2007).

In 2003 he received the Gerrit Noordzij prize from the Royal Academy in Den Haag. His type system DB Type for Deutsche Bahn (designed with Christian Schwartz) was awarded the Design Award of the Federal Republic of Germany gold medal in 2006, the highest award of its kind in Germany.

In May 2007 he was the first designer to be elected into the Hall of Fame by the European Design Awards for Communication Design. In the same year he was made an Honorary Royal Designer for Industry by the RSA in the UK. He also holds an honorary professorship at the University of the Arts Bremen and an honorary doctorate from the Pasadena Art Center. Spiekermann's books include: *Rhyme & Reason: A Typographic Novel* (1987) and *Stop Stealing Sheep and Find Out How Type Works*, with EM Ginger (1993).

FFMeta
roman *italic* SMALLCAPS old
stylefigures1234567890*ITA*
LIC SMALLCAPS lining figures
1234567890 book **medium**
boldblackcondensedbookme
dium**boldextrabold&black**

Fig 5.6

Fig 5.7

Fig 5.6: FF Meta
One of the most
successful sans serif
designs of the 1990s,
FF Meta is still going
strong today.

Fig 5.7: Sketches
Spiekermann's sketches
for FF Meta show the
essence of the typeface,
as well as details such
as the relationship
of height within the
character set.

Same face, different names

As with many aspects of our cultural lives, anything that is identified as being successful will, to some degree, have its imitators or emulators, and type is no exception. Some plainly consider it to be plagiarism. Some of the fifteenth-century types produced by Griffo for Aldus Manutius had their imitators in France shortly after they first appeared, so the problem is by no means a new one. And, as mentioned previously, the confusion over what was a real Garamond type was only corrected in the second quarter of the twentieth century.

It was in the twentieth century, however, with the development of digital image-setting technologies, that the duplication of certain well-known and established typeface designs began to appear. These were more or less exactly the same, save for their new names given by the proprietors of the new technologies.

Image-setters are high quality print output devices for producing film, bromide (paper), or direct-to-plate outputs as part of pre-press work, which is required prior to litho-printing. Many of these image-setters and related computer equipment required fonts to reside on the system. Classic or popular fonts became some of the most commonly re-appropriated designs, even if redrawn from scratch.

Arguably the first commercial digital typeface library was Bitstream. Many classic reworkings from this one foundry can still be found today. The types look identical but the names are different. Some well-known examples include Geometric 415, which was Bitstream's version of William Addison Dwiggins's 1920s Metro type; Humanist 521 = Gill Sans; and Swiss 721 = Helvetica, amongst countless others. Such types can add to the tricky job of identifying a typeface.

Garamond

Fig 5.8

Garamond

Garamond

Garamond

Garamond

Garamond

Fig 5.9

Doppelgänger
Doppelgänger

Fig 5.8: Would the real Garamond please step forward?
(From top:) Apple system Garamond; Stemple Garamond; Adobe Garamond; Monotype Garamond; Adobe Garamond 3; ITC Garamond.

Fig 5.9: Doppelgängers
Univers (top) and its doppelgänger Zurich (bottom). Adrian Frutiger's design distributed by different companies.

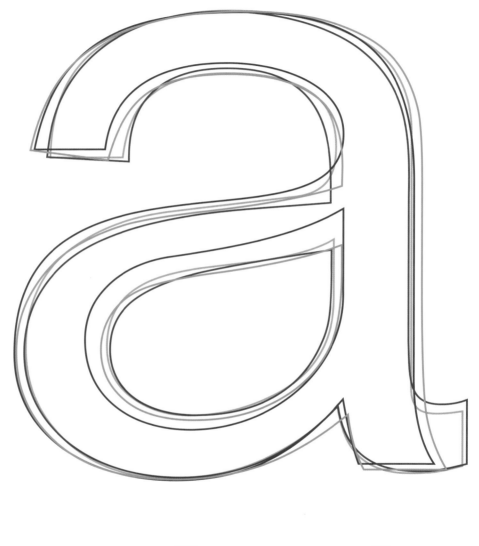

Fig 5.10

Copycats and lookalikes

As discussed, the practice of foundries releasing their own version of a type design is by no means a new phenomenon. This goes back to the earliest days of type-founding and it could be argued that if it hadn't happened, new forms and new classes of type may not have appeared at all.

The influencing factors of John Baskerville's mid-eighteenth-century types, along with the work of Fournier and Didot, culminated in the creation of the archetypal Modern typeface at the end of the century: Giambattista Bodoni's eponymously titled Bodoni. There existed various Bodoni forms, best characterized as having a strong vertical stress with a high differential in contrast between the thick and thin strokes. The flat hairline serif is also associated with Bodoni types. Bodoni is one of the most widely copied and emulated type designs in metal, photo and digital media. Many digital versions of this type suffer from overly thin strokes and hairline serifs.

In more recent history (circa 1957), typefaces such as Helvetica and Univers (which followed typefaces such as Akzidenz Grotesk) helped spawn a myriad of very closely fashioned typefaces. Just a small selection of types that afford more than a passing resemblance to the ubiquitous Helvetica include Helvetica Neue, Folio, Nimbus Sans, Chalet, Newhouse DT, Pragmatica, CG Triumvirate, Arial, Suisse BP International, New Rail Alphabet, Aktiv Grotesk and CG Heldustry. There are so many more that even spotting the most used and applied typeface on the planet is not that straightforward!

Modern
Modern
Modern
Modern
Modern

Fig 5.11

Fig 5.10: Under the influence
The variations are slight, some a little too close perhaps, but these make a huge overall difference in the distinction of the typeface.

Left to right, with colours overlaid above: Akzidenz Grotesk, Helvetica, Folio and Arial, respectively.

Fig 5.11: Modern interpretations
Again, variations on a theme. When grouped together these moderns certainly display their commonalities. Bauer Bodoni, Scotch Roman, Modern No. 20, Walbaum and Didot.

Chapter 6
Type and technology

Type and technology have always been synonymous. From its earliest beginnings type was, and continues to be, a technology. The manufacture of early lead types and the printing from these constituted standardized systems of interchangeability and reproducibility, which was truly revolutionary in terms of the development of a technology.

For over 500 years – from the time when Johannes Gutenberg brought together the making of moveable metal types, the modified press, and ink and paper – little fundamentally changed in terms of printing from metal types. Then, in the mid-1960s, phototypesetting superseded printing from metal types. Although significant, this was a fairly short-lived period in terms of the evolution of technologies related to type and typography. By the mid-1980s the advance of digital technologies, in the form of the desktop computer, saw the rapid demise of phototypesetting.

And the rest, as they say, is history…

Designers and type, together again

Today's digital technologies give type designers the ability to work directly with type designs in a way that has never been possible before. The digital outlines produced by a type designer today are the same outlines that appear within the font files on personal computers, which allows us to see more accurately how the type designer intends for a design to appear. The way in which it is reproduced, be it litho print, digital print, on screen (Internet and mobile devices) or projection, is another matter and one that earlier forms of type technology, to a great extent, did not encounter.

Much like the early punch-cutters and type founders who produced their own punches from which to make their types, today's digital type designers work directly with their own designs. However, just as in earlier times when there would be a division of labour across specialist roles, some aspects of digital type design may also require input from skilled technicians.

Such input can involve refining the drawings of types for optimal performance on different platforms, or the technical detailing of how the font file behaves as software. For example, hinting is a functionality attribute of the font software applied to glyphs so that they appear better on screen or on low-resolution printers at small sizes. Naming and packing the font, in order for it to display correctly on menus within software programs, also requires special attention. These are details that everyday users of type take for granted, but without them we would find using type in any digital context a much more difficult and unpleasant experience.

Fig 6.1

Fig 6.1: Beowolf
LettError's Beowolf
type. Random outlines
are generated from a
common base form.
Each generation of
the form is a new
interpretation.

Jeremy Tankard: digital font design

Jeremy Tankard is a British type designer with a worldwide reputation for high-quality work and unique typeface designs. A graduate of the Royal College of Art, London, Tankard began work creating and advising on typography in connection with some of the world's leading brand names.

Jeremy Tankard Typography was established in 1998, specializing in the design of new typefaces and offering bespoke typographic services and solutions to suit clients' individual needs. The company's design process begins with a rigorous approach to defining and writing a brief. The aim from the outset was to produce and license high quality digital types that maintained current standards and techniques associated with type development. Its designs are recognized as new and unique contributions within the culture of type design.

Tankard's work includes personally set typeface design challenges as well as commissioned work from clients. His personal designs include Bliss, the Shire Types, Enigma and Shaker. The work that he has undertaken for others include commissioned typefaces for Microsoft, Adobe, Zurich Airport, the FA (Football Association) and Oxford University, UK.

Tankard's work has received many awards. He has lectured widely and given workshops on typography and type design at a number of colleges and events. His work is also published in numerous books and magazines on an international level.

Fig 6.2

Fig 6.3

Fig 6.4

Trilogy Sans
Trilogy Egyptian
Trilogy Fatface
Redisturbed
Fenland

PostScript and TrueType

The most common font formats for digital types since the mid-1980s are Adobe's PostScript and Apple's TrueType. Postscript fonts began to see widespread use with the introduction of Apple's LaserWriter desktop printer in 1985. The Adobe PostScript language included Type 1 fonts that became the popular format for PostScript types. The formats of the fonts at this time were determined by the programming language used in printer output technology.

The fonts that resided on the systems of early Macintosh computers were bitmap only, which had a very limited use in terms of scaling at different sizes. Bitmap fonts became very blocky at sizes outside the range of those specifically designed. PostScript fonts, however, were interpreted from outlines and not bitmaps, which produced excellent results at all sizes on output from the printer, but not on the 72dpi screen. Individual bitmap files were supplied with PostScript fonts to try to overcome some of the rendering problems encountered on screen.

The PostScript fonts then needed two files, an outline and a bitmap. In order to get around the problem of how fonts rendered on screens at very small sizes, Adobe included hinting as part of its protected programming.

In 1991 Apple introduced TrueType, which ensured the quality of the outline and enabled scalable bitmaps from the same file. The format was licensed to Microsoft by Apple, helping to open up the Adobe-dominated font market. Then Adobe decided to publish its PostScript Type 1 information, allowing any developer to include this technology in their products. This, along with Adobe's Type Manager for the Macintosh, which allowed any Type 1 font to be scaled to any size on screen and to be anti-aliased (allowing for very smooth screen output), caused an explosion in typeface design in the mid-1990s.

PostScript and TrueType still exist today, but there is now another format, which began life in the mid-1990s, that is rapidly increasing in production and use: OpenType.

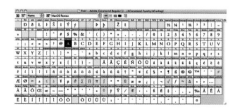

Fig 6.5

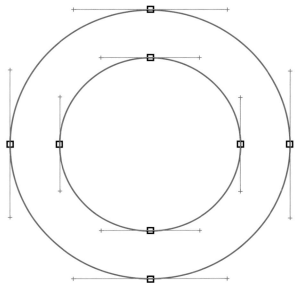

Fig 6.6

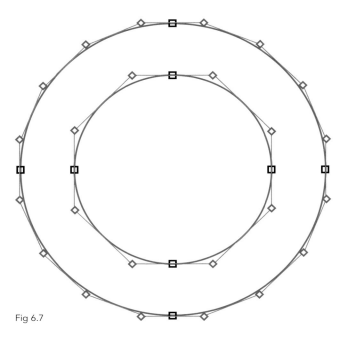

Fig 6.7

Fig 6.5: Character set
Pre OpenType, the character set for both PostScript and TrueType fonts was limited to 256 characters.

Fig 6.6–6.7: TrueType and PostScript
TrueType outlines (6.7) use quadratic bézier, on and off curve points.

PostScript outlines (6.6) use cubic bézier curves, requiring fewer points.

OpenType

OpenType is a smart font technology. It was introduced by Microsoft in 1994 as TrueType Open. It was later renamed OpenType in 1996, when it included merged support for Adobe Type 1 outlines. The outlines of TrueType fonts and PostScript Type 1 fonts can be programmed in slightly different ways to specify how the control points of the curves are generated and handled. OpenType allows for both TrueType and PostScript 'flavours' of outlines to be contained within its descriptions. For many font designers this is an important aspect of working with OpenType format as it lets them work in their preferred mode.

OpenType enables additional typographic support within compatible software programs. This can include the use of ligatures, fractions or alternative characters that would once have been supplied as an expert set alongside the regular version of a font. Extended typographic enhancement enables users to switch features on and off within the software program, in order to access different characters and so on.

In addition, because it accommodates Unicode character encoding – an agreed world standard for the representation of world language texts on computers – this means that OpenType can support up to 65,536 glyphs, making it particularly suitable for producing multiple language scripts simultaneously. There are many fonts that now have multi-language and expert characters as standard within their OpenType releases. These can be installed and used on both Macintosh and PC platforms.

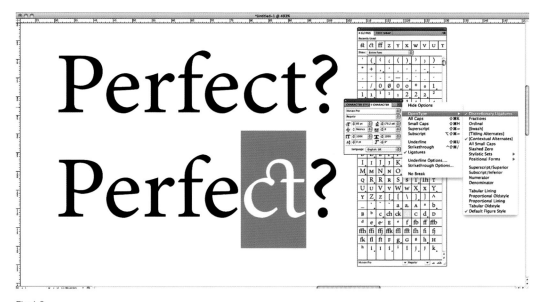

Fig 6.8

Fig 6.9

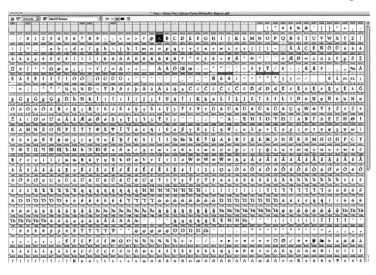

Fig 6.8: OpenType
OpenType fonts not only have an increased number of characters to allow designers to extend the number of glyphs available, working within certain software packages also allows for increased functionality of the type.

Fig 6.9: OpenType characters
An example of just half of the character map available within an OpenType font.

Web open font format (WOFF)

Just as types for the desktop computer have changed over the last three decades, so too will the way that fonts are supplied and used online in the future. One of the first big steps towards this is the WOFF or Web Open Font Format. This font format was designed for use in web pages. WOFF acts as a container and can include OpenType and TrueType font formats as well as additional information such as the font licence. This is a compressed format that produces smaller file sizes, making it ideal for use on web pages. The fact that the font licence can now be included within the font makes it an attractive option for font creators and vendors, allowing control of how fonts can be used online.

The WOFF fonts work in conjunction with special rules within web CSS (cascading style sheets) programming, called @font-face in HTML pages. This allows the pages to link to the fonts over the Internet and generate a version of the font on the user's computer. This has obvious benefits for producing rich web typography experiences for clients and users. WOFF fonts can be purchased in package agreements from websites such as Fontdeck or Typekit. Other websites, such as Font Squirrel, have sourced and gathered some of the best free or OpenSource WOFF fonts. Font Squirrel has an online @font-face generator that will allow fonts to be converted to WOFF standard. This can only be done if the terms of the font's end user licence agreement (EULA) will allow it.

'Chunk is an ultra-bold slab serif typeface that is reminiscent of old American Western woodcuts, broadsides, and newspaper headlines. Used mainly for display, the fat block lettering is unreserved yet refined for contemporary use.'

Meredith Mandel

ChunkFIVE
ABCDEF
ghijklmn
OPQRST
uvwxyz
0123456789
SLABSERIF
Meredith Mandel

Fig 6.10

Fig 6.10: Chunk
Types such as Chunk, designed by Meredith Mandel and available from The League of Moveable Type, attempt to raise the quality of free fonts available on the Internet.

OpenType functions

The use of OpenType fonts within software programs such as Adobe InDesign can add extra functionality or simply help you achieve typographic finesse within your designs.

Task

Within a program such as InDesign which will allow the application of extended OpenType functions, create a body of text type and several display size settings. Choose an OpenType font to use. This can be something like Minion Pro or Garamond Pro. You will find that the character palette has an options menu. It is here you will be able to navigate to the options for the OpenType font. Try turning on discretionary ligatures. Swash letters may be available in italic, and so on. Explore and see how this changes the nature of the type without physically loading new, extra or expert fonts to do the job.

Tip

When it comes to text, the rule of 'keep it simple' always prevails. Text with too many ligatures or swashes, although novel, just becomes irritating for the reader after a while. Explore the functions of OpenType but don't rely on them to produce automated good typography.

Fig 6.11: Applying OpenType functions
OpenType allows greater functionality and choice. However, care should be taken not to 'overwork' typography. Sometimes keeping things subtle should be the way to proceed. This sample includes small caps, ligatures, discretionary ligatures and swash capitals, yet retains a degree of subtlety.

Fig 6.11

THERE IS NOTHING SIMPLE OR DULL IN ACHIEVING THE TRANSPARENT PAGE. Vulgar ostentation is twice as easy as discipline. *When you realise that ugly typography never effaces itself;* you will be able to capture beauty as the wise men capture happiness by aiming at something else. The STUNT TYPOGRAPHER learns the *fickleness* of rich men who hate to read. Not for them are LONG BREATHS held over serif and kern, they will not appreciate your splitting of hair-spaces. *Nobody* – save the other craftsmen – will appreciate half your skill. But you may spend endless years of happy experiment in devising that *crystalline goblet* which is worthy to hold the vintage of the human mind.

BEATRICE WARDE

This book has set out to highlight and make distinct that, although connected, knowledge relating to type is not necessarily the same as knowledge relating to typography. It is useful for students and designers to be aware of these distinctions. Most students of graphic design and communication design will work with typographic matter during the development of their studies and careers.

It is hoped that the information within this book will help foster interest as well as inform readers of some of the key terminology, history, technology and figures involved in making type and in its relation to typography.

For over 500 years the essential nature of how type was produced and used in its metal form changed very little in real terms. The digital era brought us many promises of a new-found freedom in how we as designers would create and apply type in the form of typography.

Today type, in terms of its design and production and as a digital technology in itself, is becoming ever-more sophisticated. Type designs can now be delivered for multiple languages within a single font, something that was impossible only a few years ago. Fonts can also be embedded within the web pages we browse online, making for a much more pleasant reading and viewing experience. Higher resolution displays will mean that distinctions between the quality of rendering type in print, or on screen, will become negligible.

The future appears to have much in store for the development and application of type. The further this does develop, however, the more anachronistic the term 'type' becomes. The words type and typography derive from the Greek 'typos' – impression. To make an impression from type required a fixed form, in the shape of metal type, for example. In the digital world there are no fixed forms, only interpretations.

Will this mean our language appears left behind as technology increases its pace of change? The technology may change but the text it produces, the shapes and fit of the letters, the length and spacing of lines as typography, change rather more slowly.

Useful further reading

Baines P. & Haslam A. (2002) *Type and Typography*. London: Laurence King

Binns B. (1989) *Better Type*. New York: Watson-Guptill Publications

Bringhurst R. (2004) *The Elements of Typographic Style*. Point Roberts: Hartley & Marks

Carter H. (Ed.) (1930) *Fournier on Typefounding – The text of the Manuel Typographique (1764–1766) translated into English and edited with notes*. London: Soncino Press

Carter S. (1995) *Twentieth Century Type Designers*. New York: Norton

Cheng K. (2005) *Designing Type*. London: Laurence King

De Vinne T.L. (1885) *Historic Printing Types*. New York: The Grolier Club

Design Museum (2010) *How to Design a Typeface*. London: Conran Octopus

Friedl F. (1998) *Typography: When, who, how*. Konemann

Gill E. (1931/2007) *An Essay on Typography*. Jaffrey, New Hampshire: David R. Godine

Grey N. & Nash R. (1976) *Nineteenth Century Ornamented Typefaces*. New edn. London: Faber & Faber

Hochuli J. (2008) *Detail in Typography*. London: Hyphen Press

Jaspert W.P., Berry W.T. & Johnson A.F. (1983) *Encyclopaedia of Typefaces, rev. edn*. London: Blandford

Johnson A.F. (1966) *Type Designs, 3rd revised edn*. London: Andre Deutsch

Johnston E. (1935) *Writing & Illuminating & Lettering. 16th edn*. London: Pitman

Kinross R. (2008) *Modern Typography: An essay in critical history*. London: Hyphen Press

McLean R. (1980) *Thames & Hudson Manual of Typography*. London: Thames & Hudson

Meggs P. B. & McKelvey R. (2000) *Revival of the Fittest – Digital versions of classic typefaces*. New York: RC Publications

Noordzij G. (2005) *The Stroke – Theory of writing*. London: Hyphen Press

Rafaeli A. (2006) *Book Typography*. Delaware: Oak Knoll Press & London: The British Library

Ruder E. (2001) *Typographie. 7th edn*. Sulgen: Niggli Verlag

Smeijers F. (1997) *Counterpunch: Making Type in the Sixteenth Century, Designing Typefaces Now*. London: Hyphen

Spencer H. (1990) *Pioneers of Modern Typography. 2nd edn revised*. London: Lund Humphries

Spiekermann E. & Ginger E.M. (2002) *Stop Stealing Sheep and Find out how Type Works*. California: Adobe Press

Steer V. (ca 1935) *Printing Design and Layout: The Manual for Printers, Typographers and all Designers and Users of Printing and Advertising*. London: Virtue

Stienberg S.H. (1961) Five Hundred Years of Printing. 2nd edn. Middlesex: Penguin

Sutton J. & Bartram A. (1988) *An Atlas of Typeforms.* Ware: Wordsworth Editions

Tracy W. (1986) *Letters of Credit: A View of Type Design.* London: Gordon Fraser

Tschichold J. (1992) *Treasury of Alphabets and Lettering.* London: Lund Humphries

Unger G. (2005) *While You're Reading.* New York: Mark Batty

Updike D.B. (1937) *Printing Types, Their History, Forms and Use: A Study in Survivals. 2nd edn.* London: Oxford University Press

Vanderlands R., Licko Z. & Gray M.E. (1993) *Emigre – Graphic Design into the Digital Realm.* New York: Van Nostrand Reinhold

aldine

Aldine types (also see Garalde) bear a resemblance to the types utilized by Aldus Manutius. They often have an oblique stress with a more robust appearance than Venetian (or humanist) types. The crossbar of the lower-case 'e' often has a horizontal stroke. A form of 'old-style' types.

apex

The 'peak' of a letter, such as often found on the pointed top of the upper-case A.

arm

The horizontal extension of a letter, often from the vertical stem, such as found on the upper-case E, F, and L.

ascender

The part of lower-case letters that protrudes above the x-height.

ATypl

Association Typographique Internationale.

baseline

The invisible line on which the characters in a typeface sit.

bowl

The curved extension of a letter, often adjoined to an upright stem, that forms a loop with an often enclosed counter. Letters such as b, B, d, D, p, and P have bowls with counters.

bracket

Curves that connect the serif and adjoining stroke.

cap height

The height from the baseline to the top of the upper-case letters.

counter

The internal space within a type-form, often completely enclosed by a bowl. The term counter or counter-space is derived from the early process of type-founding, whereby the punch-cutter would create a 'counter-punch' in order to strike the end of a bar or rod of metal – this would form a 'counter'. It was around this 'negative' counter shape that the punch-cutter would shape the letterform for the punch.

descender

The part of a lower-case letter that descends below the baseline.

display font

A font that has been designed to work at large point sizes. These often have decorative qualities or details that may not render well at small point sizes.

finial

Often 'shaped' ending to a letter stroke/terminal.

font

A font is sometimes referred to as a collection of characters of one typeface design.

font family

A font family is sometimes referred to as a collection of characters of one typeface design and its related variants, such as roman, bold, italic and so on.

garalde

Garalde types (also see Aldine) bear a resemblance those utilized by Claude Garamond and Aldus Manutius. In general they have an oblique stress with a more robust appearance than Venetian (or humanist) types. The crossbar of the lower-case 'e' often has a horizontal stroke. A form of 'old-style' types.

glyph

Glyph is used to indicate a single character within a font. This can be a letterform, punctuation, numeral or symbol.

graphic

Graphic forms of type appear constructed or drawn rather than derived from writing or lettering in the traditional sense.

italic

A slanting or script-like variant of a typeface. Upright variants are usually referred to as 'roman'.

leg

The down-stroke found in letters such as k, K and R.

ligature

Two or more letters joined together to create a single character. For example: fi, fl, ffi, and ffl. These are often used for aesthetic purposes only. Joined characters used to indicate unique sounds, such as Æ and æ, are referred to as dipthongs.

lineal

Refers to sans serif. This also may represent the collective sub-categories of sans serif types, namely: grotesque, neo-grotesque, humanist and geometric.

'modern' typeface

Moderns are also referred to as Didones. These typefaces have a high contrast between thick and thin strokes. Characteristic is their strong vertical stress and thin, often bracket-less serifs.

oblique

A slanting version of a typeface – not the same as Italic.

OpenType

A font format that allows for larger character sets with enhanced user capabilities.

point

A unit of typographic measurement. There are approximately 72 points to one inch (2.54 cm).

point size

The measurement usually given for type. This is often the height of the 'body' upon which the letter sits.

PostScript types

Utilize Adobe's PostScript language technology. Béziers in PostScript types are cubic rather than quadratic (as found in TrueType fonts), requiring fewer points to describe curves.

roman

The upright version of a typeface.

sans serif

A typeface without serifs.

script

A typeface that often emulates less formal styles of handwritten forms. Scripts can include types based upon brush lettering, stylus and reed pen forms. They can also include precise forms such as copperplate lettering derived forms, to casual forms, such as those based upon felt-tip pen handwritten forms.

serif

Small strokes included at the terminals of the main strokes of a letter.

shoulder

The curved stroke that extends from the upright stem found in letters such as lower-case h, n and m.

slab serif

This group of typefaces emerged in the nineteenth century. These often heavy, relatively low-contrast types have a particularly mechanical appearance (often referred to as 'mechanistic' types). Their heavy serifs can appear bracketed or un-bracketed, often having a weight of stroke similar to the main strokes that make up the form of the letters.

spine

The main diagonal stroke found in letters such as lower-case 's' and upper-case 'S'.

stem

The main, often upright strokes of a letterform.

stroke

The constituent structural parts of a letterform. The term is derived from letterforms constructed by traditional writing methods, such as pen, brush, reed and stylus. The influence of the kind of writing tool and the incidence in which that would be applied in practice is considered in many typeface designs.

style

Appearance, such as italic and bold, which make up the variants of a type family.

symbol

Usually referred to as non-alphanumeric characters.

terminal

The terminating end of a stroke.

text type

Sometimes referred to as 'body-copy'. This is the continuous reading matter usually set at small sizes such as 10, 11 and 12pt.

TrueType

A standard for font outlines developed by Apple in the late 1980s. Characteristic is the use of quadratic bézier splines.

typeface

Letters, numbers, and symbols that make up a type design. A typeface can often be part of a larger family of fonts. Traditionally in metal type, the typeface was literally the design on the face of the type used as the surface to print from.

typeface family

A collection of typefaces designed to work together and usually sharing common attributes across related variants.

typographic colour

The evenness or greyness which a body of text is perceived as having. Leading, letter-spacing and word-spacing can be adjusted to alter this. Sometimes referred to as 'type texture'.

venetian

Venetian types (also humanist) are based upon the first types created in the fifteenth century by Venetian printers. These reflect the forms of formal Italian humanist handwriting of their day. Oblique stress, often less robust in form than old-style types, their serifs are often short and heavily bracketed. The crossbar of the lower-case 'e' often has a diagonal stroke.

vox

The type classification system developed by Maximilien Vox. Later to be incorporated as the Vox-ATypI classification system.

width

One possible variation of a typeface design. Condensed and expanded are width variants.

x-height

Traditionally the height of the lower-case letter x. It can also refer to the height of the body of lower-case letters, excluding the ascenders and descenders. X-heights may vary greatly in different typefaces, even at the same point size.

SWINDON COLLEGE

LEARNING RESOURCE CENTRE

Page numbers in italics refer to illustrations

Abedini, Reza *120*
additional characters 53, 160
Adobe Devanagari 79
Adobe fonts 158, 160
Akzidenz Grotesk type 28, *104*, 108
Aldine types 24, 44, 46, 170
Aldus Manutius 24, 30, *31*, 46, *115*, 146, 170, 171
Alessandrini, Jean Antoine 66
Antique type 28
apexes *34*, 170
Arabic types *73*, *81*
Archer Hairline type *107*
Ardoise type family *43*
Arial type 105
arms *34*, 170
Arrighi, Ludovico Vicentino degli 24, 46
ascenders *32–3*, *35*, 170
ATypI (Association Typographique Internationale) 64–5, 170
avant-garde movement 28, 118
awkward types 80, 84

Baines, Phil *91*
baselines *32–3*, *35*, 170
Baskerville, John 27, 118, 127, 149
Baskerville type *26*, 27, *33*
Bauermeister, Benjamin 66, *67*
Bayer, Herbert 118, *119*
Bello Pro type 123
Bembo, Pietro 30, *115*
Bembo type 24, 30, 44, *94*, 112, *115*
Beowolf type *155*
Bi Sheng 18, *19*
Bible 20, *21*
bitmap fonts 158
Bitstream (digital typeface library) 146
blackletter types *61*, 64
Bodoni, Giambattista 27, 28, 102
Bodoni type *26*, 27, 102, *103*, 149
books of samples 116, 128, *129*, *139*, 142
bowls *34–5*, 170
brackets 170
Bringhurst, Robert 66
British Standards 64–5, *65*

calligraphic types 64
  see also script types
Can You Read Me? font *89*
cap height *32–3*, 170
Carousel type *102*
Carter, Matthew 105, *107*, *113*, 114, *115*, 138
Caslon, William, I 27
Caslon, William, IV 28
Caslon type 76, *94*
Catholicon (Gutenberg type) 20
Centaur type *23*
Centro Sans type *73*
Chahine, Nadine *81*
challenging types 118, *119*
character sets *14*, 53, *158*, 160, *161*
China: early types 18, *19*
choice *see* selection of type
Chunk type 162, *163*
classic types 64, *74*, 86, 108, *109*, 128, *137*, 146
'workhorses' *110*, 111

classification 60–9, *61*, 116, 138, 140
Coe, Brian *90*
colour and type 72, *75*, *92*, 173
  see also Garamond type
Comic Sans type 105
computer fonts 13, 17, 131, 158–65, *159*
  functionality and design 105, *113*, 154
  ubiquity of defaults 86, *87*, 105
contrasting types 80, *80*, 82, *83*
copycat types 146, 149
Cottrell, William 77
counters/counter-spaces *34–5*, 108, 170
Crouwel, Wim *126*, 127

Deck, Barry *69*
Decoder type *125*
default fonts 86, *87*, 105
delicate types 106, *107*
descenders *32–3*, *35*, 170
Design Has No Name *151*
designing type 112, *113*, 124, 127, 154–7, 160
  range of types 131, 136
diacritical marks *35*, 50
Didones 62, *63*, 64, *65*, 77
Didot, Firmin 27, 102, 149
Didot type 102, *103*
digital character sets *14*, 53, 160, *161*
digital technologies 153, 158–65, 166
  experimentation and design 112, *113*, 118, 124, *125*, 154–7, 160
  online sources 124, *130*, 131, 162
  and pirate types 146
  see also computer fonts
DIN classification system 66
display types *61*, 77, 84, *89*, *96*, *97*, 170
distinguishing features 140, *141*, 150
Dixon, Catherine 66, *67*, *83*
Dolly typeface *47*
Doric type 28
Dutch types 27
Dyck, Christopher van 27

Egyptian types 28, *61*, 64, 77
Espinoza, Ramiro *122*, 123
Estienne, Robert 116, *117*
exotic types 120, *120–1*
experimental types 118, 124, 127
expert sets *52*, 53

families of fonts and type 40, 42, 48, 171, 173
  extended and super families 54, 80
  Univers family 56, *57*
fashion industry and type 102, *103*
fashions and type 102, *133*
'fat face' types 28, *29*, 76, 77
Fell types 27
Fellows, Mike 78
Fenland type 112, *156*
FF Meta type *143*, 144, *145*
finials *34*, 170
Fleischmann, Michael 27
FontBook app *12*
fonts
  definition 40, 170
  names 58, 142
  see also computer fonts; families of fonts and type; free fonts
FontShop *12*, 55, *130*, 144
Fournier, Pierre Simon 27, 127, 149
Franklin, Benjamin 27

free fonts 13, 86, *87*, *130*, 131, 162, *163*
Fregio Mecano type 127
French types 24, 27, 46
  see also Garamond type
Frutiger, Adrian 108, 136, 142
  Univers type 42, *42*, 54, 56, *57*, *147*
FSI FontShop International 144
fun types *122*, 123
Futura type 56, *85*, 118
futuristic types *126*, 127

Gaelic types 64, 65
Galliard type *115*
Garaldes 62, *63*, 64, *65*, 171
Garamond, Claude 24, 27, 48, 108, 116, *117*, 171
Garamond type 24, *25*, 108, 111, 146, *147*
  variants 48, 116, *117*, *137*
genealogies of type 39–69
genuine types 112–17
geometric types 64, 65, 118, *119*
Germany 20, 22, 66, 144
Gill sans type 32, 136
glyphic types 64, 65
glyphs 171
Gotham type *49*
Gothic types 20, 21, 22
Grandjean, Philippe 27, 127
Granjon, Robert *115*, 116
graphic types 64, 65, 171
Grecs du Roi type *117*
grid systems for type design 127
Griffo, Francesco 30–1, 44, 112, *115*, 116, 146
  italic type 24, *24*, 30, 46, *47*
Groot, Lucas de 54
Gropius, Walter 118
'grotesque' types 28, 64, 65
Guimard, Hector 11
Gutenberg, Johannes 18, 20, *21*

handwriting and type 17, 20, 44, *45*, 72
  see also script types
harmonious types 80
Helvetica type 28, *33*, 86, 105, 111, 149
hidden characters 50, *51*
Holloway, Tim 78, *79*
Humanes 62, *63*
humanist types 44, *45*, 64, 65, 173

identification issues 135–51
image-setting technologies 146
imitators 146, 149
incised types *61*, 64
Incises 62, *63*
Indian script and type 78, *79*, 120
international style 28
Internet sources 124, *130*, 131, 162
Italian types 22, 24, 30, 44, *45*, 46, *47*, 171
  see also Venetian types
italic types 24, *25*, 46, *47*
ITC Officina type *143*, 144

Jacno, Marcel 66
Jannon, Jean 48, 116
Jenson, Nicolas 22, *23*, 44

Korea: early types and books 18
Kóthay, Gábor *121*

languages: Unicode encoding 53, 160
legibility 16, 88, *89*, *91*, 108
legs *34*, 171
letterpress type trays *15*, 50
ligatures 50, *50–1*, 92, 171
lineal types 64, 65, *65*
Linéales *62*, *63*
lineals 171
Linotype: Indian script types 78, *79*
lookalikes *148*, 149
lower-case type *35*, 50

Mandel, Meredith 162, *163*
Manuaires *62*, *63*
Mécanes *62*, *63*
mechanistic types 64
MetaDesign 144
metal type *20*
Minion Pro type *110*, 111
misattribution of types 116
modern types *61*, 64, 77, 171
development *26*, *28*, *29*, 138, 149
modernism 28, 118
Monotype Bembo 30
Monotype Poliphilus 24
Morison, Stanley 24, 30, 44, *115*
Moxon, Joseph 127
MuirMcNeil *126*, 127

names of types 58–69, 142, 146
neo-grotesque types 64, *65*
newspapers *16*, 78, *79*
non-Latin types *52*, 64, *73*, 78, *79*, *81*, 120, 140
Novarese, Aldo 66

obliques 171
old-face types 44, *61*, 64, 108, 116
online sources 124, *130*, 131, 162
OpenType *52*, 53, 158, 160, *161*, 162, 164, *165*, 171
original types 112, *113*, 114

Pacioli, Fra Luca 127
Palatino, Giambattista 127
Palatino Arabic type *81*
Pannartz, Arnold 22
PANOSE classification system 66, *67*
Peignot, Charles 56
phototypesetting 153
Plantin, Christopher 116
point size 172
points 171
Porchez, Jean François *43*, *62*
PostScript fonts 53, 158, *159*, 160, 172
pro fonts *52*, 53
punch-cutting 9, 42

range of types 131, 136
readability *72*, 88, 90, *91*
Réales *62*, *63*
Redisturbed type *157*
regular types 102–11
Renner, Paul 28, *85*, 118
revival types 112, 114, *115*
Roger, Bruce *23*
Romain du Roi grid system 127
roman types 24, 44, *45*, *117*, 172
Ross, Fiona 78, *79*

Sabon, Jacques 116
samples *40*, 116, 128, *129*, *139*, 142

sans serif types 28, 86, 108, 140, 172
classification *61*, 64, 65
script types 78, *79*, 106, *107*, 172
classification *61*, *62*, *63*, 64, 65
selection of type 82, 84, 90, 92–9
identification issues 135–51
ubiquity of default fonts 86, 105
self-published types 131
serifs *34*, 36, *37*, 140, 172
shoulders *35*, 172
signage *11*, *16*, 136
size
and text type 92, *93*, *95*, 170, 173
and type families 42, 48, 54
slab serif types 28, *61*, 64, *65*, 77, 172
Slimbach, Robert 110
Snell Roundhand type *107*
sourcing type 123, 128–31, 162
specimen books 116, 128, *129*, *139*, 142
specimen sheet *40*
Spiekermann, Erik *143*, 144, *145*
spines *34*, 172
Spira, Johann and Wendelin da 22, *45*
stems *34*, 172
strokes 108, 172
thin strokes *34*, 106
style 172
super type families 54, *55*, 80
Sweynheim, Konrad 22
Swiss types 28
symbols 50, *51*, 172

Tagliente, Giovanni Antonio 46
Tankard, Jeremy 112, 156, *157*
technology and type 153–66
see also digital technologies
Template Gothic type 69
terminals *35*, *37*, 173
terminology 32–5
text types *72*, *73–5*, 84, 86, 88, *89*, 92, 173
Textura (Gutenberg type) 20, *21*
texture and type *72*, *75*, 92, 173
Thesis type family 54
Thibaudeau, Francis 62
thin strokes *34*, 106
Thorne, Robert 77
Thorowgood, William 77
ThreeSix type *126*, 127
Times New Roman type 105
titling variants *93*, 97
Tomate type *122*, 123
Tory, Geoffroy 127
transitional types *61*, 64, *65*, *65*
Trilogy type *157*
TrueType fonts 53, 158, *159*, 160, 162, 173
Tschichold, Jan 28, 118, *119*
Two Lines English Egyptian type 28, *29*
type
associations and personality *13*, 97, 98
definition 9
descriptive terminology 32–5
history and development 17, 18–31, 138
present-day usage 10–17
see also families of fonts and type
typefaces: definition *40*, 173
typography: definition 9

ubiquitous types 105
Underware *47*, 123
Unger, Gerard *125*, 136
Unicode 53, 160
unique types 118–27

Univers type 42, *42*, 54, 56, *57*, *147*, 149
Universal type 118, *119*
unusual types 124, *125*
upper-case type *34*, 50

variants 54, 58, *59*
Garamond type 48, 116, *117*, *137*
Vassilou, Panos *73*
Venetian types 22, 44, *61*, 64, 99, 173
Verdana type 105, 111, *113*
Voskens, Dirk 27
Vox classification *62*, *63*, 64, 173
Vox-ATypl classification 64–5, 140, 173

Warde, Beatrice 116, *165*
Web Open Font Format (WOFF) 162
websites and type design 124, 162
weight and type families 42, 48, 54
WhatTheFont app 138
WOFF (Web Open Font Format) 162
'workhorses' *110*, 111

x-height *32–3*, 92, *95*, 108, 173

Zanzibar type *121*
Zapf, Hermann *81*
zones *32–3*
Zurich type *147*

This book is dedicated to my father, Michael and mother, Diana.

I would like to thank all those who have allowed their work to be shown in this book.

Many thanks go to my editor Jacqui Sayers, for her understanding and support.

A special thank you goes to Helen Stallion.

And a final thank you to Lynne and Georgie for all your patience and support along the way.

All reasonable attempts have been made to trace, clear and credit the copyright holders of the images reproduced in this book. However, if any credits have been inadvertently omitted, the publisher will endeavour to incorporate amendments in future editions.

BASICS
TYPOGRAPHY

Working with ethics

Lynne Elvins
Naomi Goulder

Publisher's note

The subject of ethics is not new, yet its consideration within the applied visual arts is perhaps not as prevalent as it might be. Our aim here is to help a new generation of students, educators and practitioners find a methodology for structuring their thoughts and reflections in this vital area.

AVA Publishing hopes that these **Working with ethics** pages provide a platform for consideration and a flexible method for incorporating ethical concerns in the work of educators, students and professionals. Our approach consists of four parts:

The **introduction** is intended to be an accessible snapshot of the ethical landscape, both in terms of historical development and current dominant themes.

The **framework** positions ethical consideration into four areas and poses questions about the practical implications that might occur. Marking your response to each of these questions on the scale shown will allow your reactions to be further explored by comparison.

The **case study** sets out a real project and then poses some ethical questions for further consideration. This is a focus point for a debate rather than a critical analysis so there are no predetermined right or wrong answers.

A selection of **further reading** for you to consider areas of particular interest in more detail.

Ethical: aware-
ness/
reflect-
ion/
debate

Ethics is a complex subject that interlaces the idea of responsibilities to society with a wide range of considerations relevant to the character and happiness of the individual. It concerns virtues of compassion, loyalty and strength, but also of confidence, imagination, humour and optimism. As introduced in ancient Greek philosophy, the fundamental ethical question is: *what should I do?* How we might pursue a 'good' life not only raises moral concerns about the effects of our actions on others, but also personal concerns about our own integrity.

In modern times the most important and controversial questions in ethics have been the moral ones. With growing populations and improvements in mobility and communications, it is not surprising that considerations about how to structure our lives together on the planet should come to the forefront. For visual artists and communicators, it should be no surprise that these considerations will enter into the creative process.

Some ethical considerations are already enshrined in government laws and regulations or in professional codes of conduct. For example, plagiarism and breaches of confidentiality can be punishable offences. Legislation in various nations makes it unlawful to exclude people with disabilities from accessing information or spaces. The trade of ivory as a material has been banned in many countries. In these cases, a clear line has been drawn under what is unacceptable.

But most ethical matters remain open to debate, among experts and lay-people alike, and in the end we have to make our own choices on the basis of our own guiding principles or values.

Is it more ethical to work for a charity than for a commercial company? Is it unethical to create something that others find ugly or offensive?

Specific questions such as these may lead to other questions that are more abstract. For example, is it only effects on humans (and what they care about) that are important, or might effects on the natural world require attention too?

Is promoting ethical consequences justified even when it requires ethical sacrifices along the way? Must there be a single unifying theory of ethics (such as the Utilitarian thesis that the right course of action is always the one that leads to the greatest happiness of the greatest number), or might there always be many different ethical values that pull a person in various directions?

As we enter into ethical debate and engage with these dilemmas on a personal and professional level, we may change our views or change our view of others. The real test though is whether, as we reflect on these matters, we change the way we act as well as the way we think. Socrates, the 'father' of philosophy, proposed that people will naturally do 'good' if they know what is right. But this point might only lead us to yet another question: *how do we know what is right?*

You
What are your ethical beliefs?

Central to everything you do will be your attitude to people and issues around you. For some people, their ethics are an active part of the decisions they make every day as a consumer, a voter or a working professional. Others may think about ethics very little and yet this does not automatically make them unethical. Personal beliefs, lifestyle, politics, nationality, religion, gender, class or education can all influence your ethical viewpoint.

Using the scale, where would you place yourself? What do you take into account to make your decision? Compare results with your friends or colleagues.

Your client
What are your terms?

Working relationships are central to whether ethics can be embedded into a project, and your conduct on a day-to-day basis is a demonstration of your professional ethics. The decision with the biggest impact is whom you choose to work with in the first place. Cigarette companies or arms traders are often-cited examples when talking about where a line might be drawn, but rarely are real situations so extreme. At what point might you turn down a project on ethical grounds and how much does the reality of having to earn a living affect your ability to choose?

Using the scale, where would you place a project? How does this compare to your personal ethical level?

01 02 03 04 05 06 07 08 09 10

01 02 03 04 05 06 07 08 09 10

Your specifications
What are the impacts of your materials?

In relatively recent times, we are learning that many natural materials are in short supply. At the same time, we are increasingly aware that some man-made materials can have harmful, long-term effects on people or the planet. How much do you know about the materials that you use? Do you know where they come from, how far they travel and under what conditions they are obtained? When your creation is no longer needed, will it be easy and safe to recycle? Will it disappear without a trace? Are these considerations your responsibility or are they out of your hands?

Using the scale, mark how ethical your material choices are.

Your creation
What is the purpose of your work?

Between you, your colleagues and an agreed brief, what will your creation achieve? What purpose will it have in society and will it make a positive contribution? Should your work result in more than commercial success or industry awards? Might your creation help save lives, educate, protect or inspire? Form and function are two established aspects of judging a creation, but there is little consensus on the obligations of visual artists and communicators toward society, or the role they might have in solving social or environmental problems. If you want recognition for being the creator, how responsible are you for what you create and where might that responsibility end?

Using the scale, mark how ethical the purpose of your work is.

01 02 03 04 05 06 07 08 09 10

01 02 03 04 05 06 07 08 09 10

An aspect of typography that may raise ethical issues is its capacity to make information accessible or understandable to the reader. Creative use of typography can emphasise meaning and embed emotion in words. In this way, typography can facilitate verbal and visual communication, and in turn give rise to fundamental questions about the role of a given piece of text.

Will the text instruct, inform or helpfully guide the receiver towards beneficial information of some kind? Or might it confuse, frighten or alienate all but a select few? Does a typographer have a responsibility to always be as clear, informative and legible as possible? Or are there occasions where the decorative treatment of script is far more important than the ability to read the words? How much responsibility should the typographer assume for the message, as well as for the means by which it is delivered?

Graffiti has been found around the world and throughout history, from the catacombs of Rome to the Mayan temple walls of Tikal in Mesoamerica. Graffiti found in Pompeii, with its messages of political rhetoric or Latin curses, provides us with insights into the daily lives of people during the first century. Graffiti continues to tell us about life today, as well as directly reflecting the writer's views of society.

In France during the student protests and general strike of May 1968, revolutionary anarchist and situationist slogans covered the walls of Paris, articulating the spirit of the age. In the US, around the same time, street gangs were using graffiti as a means to mark territory. Signatures or 'tags', rather than slogans, were used by writers such as TOPCAT 126 and COOL EARL. CORNBREAD, credited by some as the father of modern graffiti, began his career by writing 'Cornbread loves Cynthia' all over his school. In the early 1970s, graffiti moved to New York and writers such as TAKI 183 began to add their street number to their nickname. Tags began to take on a calligraphic appearance in order to stand out, and also began to grow in size and include thick outlines. Bubble lettering was initially popular before 'wildstyle' – a complicated creation of interlocking letters using lots of arrows and connections – came to define the art of graffiti.

The use of graffiti as a portrayal of rebellious urban style made it attractive to creatives operating within mainstream culture. In 2001, fashion designer and artist Stephen Sprouse, in collaboration with fellow designer Marc Jacobs, designed a limited-edition line of Louis Vuitton bags that featured graffiti scrawled over the company's monogrammed pattern.

Despite the fact that graffiti has now become both a familiar and accepted artistic form within everyday society, it remains controversial. There is a clear distinction between graffiti employed typographically by a designer or artist, to graffiti that is applied to either public or private property. In most countries, defacing property without permission is deemed to be vandalism and is therefore punishable by law. Governments spend vast sums of public money removing graffiti. A 1995 study by the National Graffiti Information Network estimated that the cost of cleaning up graffiti in the US amounted annually to approximately USD 8 billion.

If it is illegal, is it also unethical to graffiti on someone else's property?

Are companies exploiting graffiti if they use it to sell commercial goods?

Would you be prepared to be imprisoned to communicate a message?

A word is not a crystal, transparent and unchanged; it is the skin of a living thought, and may vary greatly in color and content according to the circumstances and the time in which it is used.

Oliver Wendell Holmes Jr

AIGA
Design Business and Ethics
2007, AIGA

Eaton, M.M.
Aesthetics and the Good Life
1989, Associated University Press

Ellison, D.
Ethics and Aesthetics in European Modernist Literature:
From the Sublime to the Uncanny
2001, Cambridge University Press

Fenner, D.E.W. (Ed)
Ethics and the Arts:
An Anthology
1995, Garland Reference Library of Social Science

Gini, A. and M., Alexei M.
Case Studies in Business Ethics
2005, Prentice Hall

McDonough, W. and Braungart, M.
Cradle to Cradle:
Remaking the Way We Make Things
2002, North Point Press

Papanek, V.
Design for the Real World:
Making to Measure
1972, Thames & Hudson

United Nations Global Compact
The Ten Principles
www.unglobalcompact.org/AboutTheGC/TheTenPrinciples/index.html